SQUADRONS!

No. 69

THE NORTH AMERICAN
MITCHELL
- THE RAF IN THE FAR EAST, THE NEIAF & THE RAAF -

PHIL H. LISTEMANN

ISBN: 9782494471-22-1

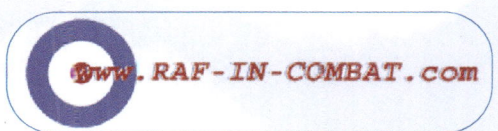

www.RAF-IN-COMBAT.com

Colour profiles: Gaetan Marie/Bravo Bravo Aviation

GLOSSARY OF TERMS

PERSONEL :

(AUS)/RAF: Australian serving in the RAF
(BEL)/RAF: Belgian serving in the RAF
(CAN)/RAF: Canadian serving in the RAF
(CZ)/RAF: Czechoslovak serving in the RAF
(NFL)/RAF: Newfoundlander serving in the RAF
(NL)/RAF: Dutch serving in the RAF
(NZ)/RAF: New Zealander serving in the RAF
(POL)/RAF: Pole serving in the RAF
(RHO)/RAF: Rhodesian serving in the RAF
(SA)/RAF: South African serving in the RAF
(US)/RAF - RCAF : American serving in the RAF or RCAF

RANKS

G/C : Group Captain
W/C : Wing Commander
S/L : Squadron Leader
F/L : Flight Lieutenant
F/O : Flying Officer
P/O : Pilot Officer
W/O : Warrant Officer
F/Sgt : Flight Sergeant
Sgt : Sergeant
Cpl : Corporal
LAC : Leading Aircraftman

OTHER

ATA: Air Transport Auxiliary
CO : Commander
DFC : Distinguished Flying Cross
DFM : Distinguished Flying Medal
DSO : Distinguished Service Order
Eva. : Evaded
ORB : Operational Record Book
OTU : Operational Training Unit
PoW : Prisoner of War
PAF: Polish Air Force
RAF : Royal Air Force
RAAF : Royal Australian Air Force
RCAF : Royal Canadian Air Force
RNZAF : Royal New Zealand Air Force
SAAF : South African Air Force
s/d: Shot down
Sqn : Squadron
† : Killed

THE N.A. MITCHELL

The Mitchell was ordered 'off the drawing board' in September 1939, being a development of North American's NA-40 conceived in 1938. There was no 'XB-25'; the first B-25 made its maiden flight on 19 August 1940 powered by two 1,700-hp Wright Cyclone engines. The B-25As which followed were similar apart from some internal improvements; 40 of this version had been completed, and were in service, at the time of the attack on Pearl Harbor. Production of the 119 B-25Bs, which incorporated armament changes, was underway and although this version became famous for its participation in the Tokyo raid, it was not really combat ready. It was soon followed by the B-25C (built at Inglewood, California) and D (built at Kansas City, Montana) which were largely similar, apart from the engines and further internal changes. These two versions were widely used until the end of the war and, ultimately, 1 619 B-25Cs and 2,290 B-25Ds were completed.

The B-25 Mitchell, unlike its competitor, the Martin B-26 Marauder, was widely exported. Deliveries were made to the air forces of the United Kingdom, Soviet Union, the Netherlands, Brazil, Canada and Australia. The US Marine Corps introduced its own version under the PBJ denomination and saw action in the Pacific. These conventional bomber versions were followed by the specialised B-25G (405 produced). This was equipped with the famous 75-mm cannon carried in a 'solid' nose. The 1,000 B-25Hs which followed were an improved version utilising a lighter 75-mm cannon, together with fourteen 0.50 machine-guns and provision for a torpedo or 3,200 lb of bombs, making this Mitchell one of the most heavily armed aircraft in the world at the time. The 75-mm cannon was gradually phased out of service during the war in favour of the more reliable and ubiquitous machine guns.

In the early weeks of 1944, a new version, the B-25J, was introduced and became the principal version of the Mitchell. It was in production from late 1943 to the end of the war, by which time 4,318 had been completed. Production ceased after VJ-Day. This model reverted to the bombing role but, apart from its transparent nose, and modified armament, it was similar to the B-25H. Like earlier versions, some B-25Js were subsequently modified in the field to have a 'solid' eight machine-gun nose for ground attack (this was supplied by North American as a kit and then introduced on the production line). The B-25 was the most widely used Allied medium bomber during WW2 and saw action on all fronts.

A line-up of Mitchells wearing various national markings at the Inglewood facilities in the beginning of 1942. In the foreground can be seen US markings and behind are aircraft for countries supplied via the Lend-Lease programme: the USSR, the Netherlands and Britain. Note the serial N5-126 and the orange triangle on the Dutch machine. The NEI surrendered soon after and no Dutch B-25 would ever fly operations carrying the orange triangle.

A line-up of Dutch B-25s in new markings at Canberra, Australia, in the late spring of 1942. N5-132 was soon issued to No. 18 (NEI) Squadron.

During the war, the Mitchell, under the denomination of 'AT-24', proved a good training aircraft; nearly 1,000 were thus converted after the war, while others were converted to staff transports or handed over to a number of Latin American countries which used them as bombers well into the 1950s.

THE DUTCH CONNECTION

The presence of the Mitchell in the South-West Pacific and the Far East in non-US markings had its origin with the Dutch. On 30 June 1941, the Netherlands Purchasing Commission (NPC) ordered 162 B-25Cs to be used in the Netherlands East Indies (NEI). This purchase was eventually approved by an American government that was at first reluctant but wanted to reinforce potential allies in the face of the increasing threat of an expanding Japanese empire. The aircraft were paid for in cash and the batch received the North American denomination of NA-90. Deliveries were scheduled to start in November 1942 and be completed in February 1943 (25 that month, 50 in December, 80 in January and 7 in February), with serials **N5-122 to N5-283** (coinciding with USAAF serials 42-53332 to 53493), but the delivery of B-25s on order for the USAAF had to take precedence. However, when war reached South-East Asia in December 1941, the NPC requested an accelerated delivery plan that was duly accepted; the Dutch were to see six B-25s delivered each month between March and September 1942, 18 in October and November, then 36 in December 1942 and January 1943, with the last 12 arriving in February. To make those deliveries possible, aircraft destined for American service, and therefore built earlier, were exchanged with the original airframes intended for the NEI.

When the NEI fell in March 1942, the first Mitchells were already on their way. About 28 aircraft were eventually diverted to Australia; their presence would lead to the formation of No. 18 (NEI) Squadron RAAF later in the year although some were immediately impressed by the USAAF. More Dutch Mitchells arrived in Australia although it soon became clear there would not be enough Dutch crews to make use of the 162 aircraft ordered. Some aircraft were later transferred to the RAAF to convert No. 2 Squadron RAAF on to the type but, even with that, there were still too many Mitchells. The US government offered to divert a part of the order to the UK where other Dutch aircrew were fighting with the RAF, but there was only one operational squadron, No. 320 (Dutch) Squadron, which had formed in June 1940 with former Royal Netherlands Naval Air Service (RNNAS) personnel evacuated to Britain (see *SQUADRONS! 16*).

In Australia, a group consisting of 18 pilots, seven telegraphers and 14 mechanics, under the leadership of *Kaptain* Boot, was available. The first Mitchell arrived at Archerfield airfield in Queensland on 2 March 1942. These 18 B-25Cs were part of a batch of 60 aircraft to be sent to Australia.

The first 12 B-25s wore 'N5' serials and orange triangles. According to photos, the serials were N5-120 to N5-131. The Mitchells flying via India (see below) are thought to have been registered N5-139 to N5-148. The second batch of 24 aircraft arrived in March and April 1942. This batch was handed over to the USAAF as already agreed. The Dutch were to receive 60 Mitchells in Australia plus the six delivered in India (one crashed on its way) for a total of 66 aircraft. It was agreed that, of these 60 Mitchells, 42 had to be handed over to the USAAF, inclusive of those already delivered. So, 18 Mitchells were left for the Dutch in Australia.

When the Dutch purchased the B-25, it was the intention to send half of the aircraft via India. The first batch of 12 was allocated serials N5-137 through -148 and were to be ferried via Brazil and the colony of Gold Coast in West Africa. On 26 February 1942, the first five of the first batch left the USA, followed on 1 March by the sixth aircraft. However, with the situation in the NEI now desperate, it was decided the same day to not send further B-25s to India. Therefore, the second batch was sent directly to Australia. The first B-25 arrived at Bangalore on 8 March and the last ones landed on 17 March. Only five B-25s made the flight as N5-140 crashed while landing at Acca, Gold Coast, the British crew losing their lives. The remaining five B-25s, which arrived safely in India, were N5-139, 143, 144, 145 and 148. Coming from the NEI, a detachment of personnel from the Netherlands East Indies Air Force arrived from Java soon after under the command of Kapt R Wittert van Hoogland. They received ground instruction from the ferry crews and Lt P.C. André de la Porte initiated the first test flight. After the fall of Java, the fate of the Dutch personnel and the five B-25s was uncertain. As the RAF was also in a bad situation in the region and in urgent need of aircraft, a deal was made and it was decided in mid-April to use the B-25s as reconnaissance platforms with No. 3 Photographic Reconnaissance Unit, to be reformed on 13 May under the leadership of W/C S.G. Wise. Consequently, the five B-25s were sent to Karachi for modifications; cameras were installed and RAF roundels applied as well as new paint. Only the Dutch serials were maintained. All the aircraft were modified by 1 May.

Initially based at Pandaveswar, 3 PRU moved to Dum Dum on 28 June. In the meantime, the first photo recce was carried out on 2 June by F/L J.D. Thirwell and crew. The op was to take photos of Toungoo, Lampang and Chienguai, but was abandoned off the Indian coast due to engine trouble. The next sortie, flown on 6 June by F/O J.K. Edmonds, was a success, however, and photos were taken of the objective. Eight more sorties were flown in June, but two accidents obliged the RAF to put a stop to proceedings. On 22 June, N5-139/E suffered a punctured tyre while landing after a practice flight. As there were no replacement tyres available for the B-25s at the time, N5-139 was left at the side of the runway. However, during the night, a Hurricane collided with the B-25 on landing, cutting into the fuselage at the mid-turret position so that it collapsed with the tail unit on the ground. A few days later, N5-143/D had one of its engines catch fire immediately after take-off for a sortie to the Andaman Islands; an emergency ditching was made in the three-foot deep mid-channel of the nearby Ajay River. N5-139 was eventually repaired, using parts from N5-143, and would be collected in November. Still based at Dum Dum, operations resumed in August, although the monsoon only allowed for four sorties to be carried out during the month, with seven more in September and four in October. On 8 August, Lt Van Rooyan (SAAF) was intercepted by two Japanese Ki-27s that inflicted some damage, but the Mitchell managed to escape. The Mitchells were called upon more often in November and December with 12 and 14 sorties flown respectively but, again, the weather had the final say. The Mitchells were focussing on the Andaman Islands and Rangoon area as the British feared a naval operation could be mounted against eastern India and Ceylon. Fifteen more sorties were performed in January up to the 25[h] when 3 PRU was re-dominated No 681 Squadron; Wise remained the CO and the Mitchells formed C Flight. Three of them, N5-148/A, N5-144/B, N5-145/C, were still operational with a spare (N5-139/E) mainly used for training or liaison purposes. The recces otherwise remained the same – 17 sorties were carried out in January 1943. The Mitchell, after a difficult debut, now enjoyed a good safety record but, on 13 February, N5-148/A, which had taken off for a photographic reconnaissance over Burma, failed to return; the entire crew, led by F/O R.L .Barnett, an American serving with the RAF, was posted missing. C Flight was now obliged to soldier on with two Mitchells. N5-144/B and N5-145/C did the job and were soon reinforced by two Mitchells transferred from the USAAF in India – MA956/E (ex B-25C-NA 41-12666) and MA957/K (ex B-25C-NA 41-12659) – which arrived in July 1943 after their PR conversion. The new aircraft assumed the duties of the former Dutch Mitchells while the older aircraft received a much-needed overhaul. From August up to 1 November, 17 sorties were carried out for a grand total of 155 since the first one in June 1942. That day, 1 November, No. 684 Squadron was formed at Dum Dum and C Flight with its Mitchells was transferred to fly alongside the Mosquitos of the squadron's other flight. This new unit was also a PR unit but was only equipped with

The former Dutch N5-148/A while serving with 3 PRU in 1943. Used as a photographic reconnaissance aircraft, the dorsal turret was removed on all Mitchells of this unit to save weight and increase speed in case of interception. The B-25 was the only long-range photo aircraft of the RAF in India until the arrival of the Mosquito.

twin-engine machines, leaving 681 flying single-engine aircraft. At this period of the war, the Mosquito was a better aircraft for the job and could easily do what the Mitchell was only just able to do – reach Rangoon. The Mitchell was no longer seen as the main equipment for the role. The type's usage remained limited in the following weeks, with eight operational flights performed in November and four in December. In January 1944, only two sorties were flown. At the end of 1943, the Air Ministry agreed to provide 20 Mosquito PRs during early 1944, announcing at the same time the pending end of the Mitchell as a PR machine in the Far East. On 9 December, 684 moved to Comilla, only to return to Dum Dum on 31 January 1944. It then moved to Alipore on 5 May. By that time, the Mitchells had already been relegated and were serving in secondary tasks, mainly to transport material, senior officers or squadron personnel, and deliver photographic prints to forward areas. Normally, this task should have been given to specific aircraft allocated to the squadron but short supply in the Far East forced the hands of 684's staff. Now kept in reserve, some of the Mitchells had their individual letter changed. After March 1944, 684 had on strength N5-145/Z and MA957/X, the only two still capable of flying operational PR sorties; several would be flown during the year. The other airframes, MA956/E and N5-144/B, were soon stripped of any operational equipment to serve as transports. About 20 sorties were nevertheless flown in 1944. Sometimes the Mitchells were called upon to fly other sorties, like air–sea rescue. On 5 November 1944, it was during one such mission that MA957/X was lost with its crew of four. Soon after, on 15 December, MA956/E was damaged by fire during a routine inspection and the nose section distorted beyond the repair capability of the squadron. Only N5-145/Z was therefore left serviceable to soldier on in non-operational duties until May 1945, achieving 80 hours of flight in the first four months of the year.

Summary of the aircraft lost on Operations with the RAF

Date	Crew	S/N	Origin	Serial	Code	Fate
13.02.43	F/O Redmond L. **Barnett**	RAF No. 111237	(US)/RAF	N5-148	A	†
	F/O Michael J. **Hobsey**	RAF No. 61497	RAF			†
	W/O Henry A. **Brindle**	SAAF No. 580360	SAAF			†
	LAC Benjamin **Weighell**	RAF No. 1253670	RAF			†
05.11.44	F/L Neil **Robison**	RAF No. 109915	RAF	MA957	X	†
	F/L Desmond J. **Sutcliffe**	RAF No. 123501	RAF			†
	F/O Benjamin **Redfern**	RAF No. 141947	RAF			†
	LAC Ronald S. **Bury**	RAF No. 1522216	RAF			†

Total: 2

B-25 N5-145/Z at dispersal with No. 684 Squadron towards the end of the operational service of the PR Mitchell in the RAF.
(Andrew Thomas)

Number of sorties: *ca.* 2,400

First operational sortie:
05.06.42

Number of claims: 6.0

Last operational sortie:
29.04.45

Total aircraft written-off: 24

Aircraft lost on operations: 18
Aircraft lost in accidents: 6

Squadron code letters:
-

COMMANDING OFFICERS

Kapt W. BOOT *(Temp.)*	NEIAF	21.04.42	01.05.42
Lt-Kol Bernard FIEDELDIJ	NEIAF	01.05.42	11.06.43
Lt-Kol Jacobius ZOMER	NEIAF	11.06.44	01.04.44
Lt-Kol Everhardus TE ROLLER *(†)*	NEIAF	01.04.44	23.06.44
Lt-Kol Dirk ASJES	NEAIF	01.07.44	07.10.44
Lt-Kol Marinus VAN HASELEN	NEIAF	07.10.44	13.06.45
Lt-Kol Reiner JESSURUM	NEIAF	13.06.45	...

SQUADRON USAGE

Formed at Canberra in Australia on 4 April 1942 as a bomber squadron, the Americans supplied all of No. 18 Squadron's stores and equipment while the personnel were drawn from the Dutch Detachment at Archerfield, and from the NEI Transport Group and other personnel gathered in Melbourne. This was still far from enough, however, and the RAAF was obliged to provide personnel to complete the establishment for aircrew (mostly air gunners) and ground staff. Command was given to Maj Bernardus Fiedeldij, who arrived on 21 April and officially took over on 1 May. From the start, the new unit faced a lack of aircraft. It was initially planned to receive 18 Mitchells from the Dutch order, but these first Dutch machines were immediately rushed to the USAAF in the Pacific to be used by the 3rd Bomb Group. Only four aircraft remained (N5-132, 134, 136 and 161), on which training could be undertaken. To resolve the problem, conversion to the Douglas Boston, using an ex-Dutch Navy batch diverted to Australia after the fall of the NEI, was considered. Some were received in June, but the idea was soon abandoned and the aircraft were eventually transferred to No. 22 Squadron RAAF (see *SQUADRONS!* 22). In the meantime, the presence of three midget Japanese submarines in Sydney Harbour on 31 May resulted in a widespread panic and the squadron, despite not yet being operational, was rushed into action on 5 June

Bernardus Fiedeldij joined the Dutch Army Air Force in 1929. He trained as a pilot and was commissioned as a second lieutenant in 1931. He was assigned to the Dutch East Indies in 1934 and served there until 1939. When the Japanese invaded in 1942, Fiedeldij was evacuated to Australia. Owing to his experience, he was given the command of No. 18 (NEI) Squadron upon its formation on 21 April, leading the squadron through its initial stage of operations. After the war, he served in the new RNethAF until he retired in 1954.

One of the first B-25s allotted to the Dutch squadron, N5-137 still wears its US serial on the tail.

to carry out anti-submarine patrols. On the very first day, it flew five sorties; the crew under the command of 2/Lt W Winckel succeeded in sinking a Japanese midget submarine in coastal waters near Sydney. Over the next few days, 26 more patrols were flown; this period of activity was closed out on 12 June with an uneventful convoy escort. In the first few days of July, the existing Mitchells were re-registered as so many out-of-sequence numbers, due to partial deliveries, proved confusing. The new series started with N5-122 (ex-N5-132). The others received serials N5-123 (ex-N5-134), N5-124 (ex-N5-136), N5-125 (ex-N5-151) and N5-126 (ex-N5-161); the B-25C received on 30 June, N5-146, became N5-127. Anti-submarine patrols resumed in the closing days of July, the squadron occasionally using the airstrips at Moruya and Jervis Bay. One sortie ended badly way for 1/Lt Jansen and his crew when the undercarriage of N5-126 malfunctioned on return from a patrol. The subsequent crash landing at Moruya badly damaged the B-25, which was sent out for repairs. Fortunately, the crew was safe. On 22 August, 18 Squadron took charge of five new B-25Cs still wearing their US serials (12914, 12916, 12919, 12936 and 29713), which soon received the NEI serials N5-130, N5-129, N5-132, N5-131 and N5-133 respectively. Over the following days, going well into September, a turnover of aircraft took place. N5-123, 124, 125 and 127 were handed over to the Americans while N5-134, 135, 136, 137 and 138 were taken on charge, later followed by N5-140 and 141, and N5-142 and 143, N5-139, N5-144 and N5-145. The squadron remained at Canberra until 5 December when it moved to McDonald in the Northern Territory. During its stay at Canberra, the unit continued training and increased its personnel strength. It was also highly publicized and participated in various parades to show the Dutch were fighting alongside the Allies, but this long period of inactivity had a bad impact on morale. To restore morale, some brutal action was undertaken in mid-November against some aircrew who were planning to desert and return to Java in a B-25. That event shocked the rest of the squadron, the move to the Northern Territory being seen as fortuitous (or maybe it was simply a way to get the squadron on track). The move and settling in at McDonald took the entire month and the beginning of January 1943. Ignoring the emergency landing of N5-133, flown by 1/Lt AF Oudraad, due to bad weather, the move was completed successfully (Oudraad's Mitchell would eventually rejoin the squadron later in January). At McDonald, the squadron was placed under RAAF command and, from 11 January, each crew managed to reconnoiter the vicinity, getting in more practice in the process. The 'real' start came on 18 January when a reconnaissance flight was carried out from Darwin to find enemy shipping near the Tanimbar Islands. The next day, another was flown to the Toeal and Kei Islands; nothing was found but the alternate target was attacked, N5-143 obtaining three hits and N5-144 four in using their front guns. More offensive shipping recces were carried out the next day; the formation was intercepted by five 'Zekes' between Darwin and Sermati and the island of Kisar. The B-25s sustained no damage but two 'Zekes' were claimed as probably destroyed by the gunners who saw them break off pouring smoke. Each B-25 fired 380 rounds. The same day, the first bombs were also dropped. Three days later, near Timor, the Mitchells were attacked by a single Japanese fighter that made several passes without success. The same applied to the Dutch despite 800 rounds being fired at the attacking aircraft. Now the squadron was really at war. On the last day of the month, it avoided a major setback . That day, Flight No 2 (N5-129, N5-132 and N5-137) and Flight No.4 (N5-134, N5-135 and N5-139) made a dawn attack on Dilli on ships and the airfield. There was zero visibility over the target. There were no enemy sightings, no interception by the enemy and Nil bombs were dropped. On return N5-134 (1/Lt Cooke) made a forced landing on the runway at Ports Keats due to a shortage of fuel. There was no injuries or damage to the aircraft. However, N5-139 (S/Maj de Jongh) made a forced landing in marsh ground due to a shortage of fuel as well. If

Three early B-25s, with N5-139 and 140 visible, on training flights.

the crew was rescued, N5-139 was left behind. In February, the tempo of sorties increased with about 40 carried out and various targets attacked. The squadron paid for this increase in activity; on 5 February, while taking off for Darwin with three other aircraft to be on readiness there, the Mitchell flown by S/Maj L Schalk crashed with a full bomb load. The crew of five, including two Australians, and four Dutch mechanics all died. Despite the quick intervention of the rescue team, the only survivor of the crash, Sgt Walton (RAAF), died while being transported to hospital. More casualties were reported later on 18 February during an attack on a heavily camouflaged ship in the harbour at Dili. No hits were recorded and the Mitchells experienced heavy anti-aircraft fire from the ship and ground positions, although none was hit. Soon after, five 'Zekes' intercepted the bombers. The running fight lasted 45 long minutes, the Dutch claiming one of the attackers destroyed and another as damaged. The Japanese got hits too: N5-144, captained by 2/Lt BJ Grummels, was hit in the left engine which had to be shut down. Having flown about 20 miles, maintaining the Mitchell in flight became too difficult and Grummels was forced to ditch. Two of the crew, Grummels and Sgt RG Tyler of the RAAF, perished. The others, all injured to some degree, were rescued; Australian F/Sgt RS Hooridge was the most seriously wounded. In March, the squadron maintained the rhythm of operations but added lonely reconnaissance sorties to their duties. That month, another 'Zeke' was claimed as probably destroyed by the gunners on N5-140 (captained by S/Maj Tijmons) during an attack on the airstrip at Fuiloro in Portuguese Timor on the 12th, while the gunners of N5-137 (Lt Hagers) claimed one more as destroyed but the Mitchell was damaged in return and the upper gunner, Sgt CW Hutchinson (RAAF), was also injured. The Dutch would claim another 'Zeke' destroyed on 30 March during a reconnaissance made by N5-133, captained by Lt Swain, of the Kaimana district and south of Cape Van Den Bosch. The Mitchell at first attacked six vessels sighted; during the bombing run, it was damaged by flak. Soon after, two 'Zekes' showed up and attacked. One was soon shot down in flames from a distance of 50 yards, the pilot baling out, while the second was damaged. The two fighters managed to score hits on the B-25, however, and the right engine had to be shut down. Swain managed to reach Australia but was obliged to make a forced landing at Point Jahleel, the most northern point of Melville Island; 1/Lt de Wolf was injured. The crew was eventually rescued on 1 April, but the B-25 was not salvageable.

In April, the squadron began to move to Batchelor in the Northern Territory, the targets assigned being located in Timor, Ambon, and the Kai and Aore Islands to stop seaborne traffic. Before the move was made, however, the Mitchell captained by S/Maj G Tijmons was lost during an evening take-off for an armed recce; all the crew, including two Australians, perished. The two other Mitchells completed their duty without incident. Another crew comprising two Australians was lost on 28 April, shot down by anti-aircraft fire from the ships four Mitchells were attacking. To make up for attrition, new aircraft were taken on charge in April – N5-146 and 147, then N5-

148, 149, 150, 151 and 152 while N5-153 followed soon after. In April, the squadron was involved in more and more anti-shipping operations at mast height and, the following month, the aircraft began to receive field mods to make them more effective during such attacks. The first modifications included two extra forward-firing machine guns located on both sides of the fuselage in gun packs; part of this work included strengthening the nose structure. At the same time, the extra tanks fitted in the bomb bay in December were removed so the whole bay could be used for its original purpose. The squadron continued to use unmodified Mitchells in the anti-shipping role while, from 10 May, the move to Batchelor was completed. Three Mitchells were lost in May and June: N5-147 on 21 May, N5-152 the next day, and N5-150 on 2 June. N5-147 was shot down by anti-aircraft fire while making a bombing attack on Saumalakki and crashed into the sea. One parachute was observed and was last seen floating towards the water about 11 miles from where the B-25 crashed. Later, Japanese broadcast claimed the commander of this aircraft, likely 2/Lt L. Bal had been captured and became a PoW. Postwar interrogations suggest that two Dutch Lieutenants from this aircraft may have been captured. That means that 1/Lt P Kruijne possibly survived too. However, the fates of these prisoners is unknown. Likely they died of neglect or were executed.

The next day, N5-152 crashed on take-off after an engine failure. Kaptain R Jessurun, who was in the observer's compartment, was seriously injured in the subsequent crash but the rest of the crew escaped almost unscathed. N5-150 simply failed to return from an operation against shipping off Timor and was last seen heading towards the Timor mainland through thick weather. The crew of five, including three Australians, was posted missing. At the same time, armed reconnaissance flights became the norm and were allocated code names like 'Search Giraffe' or 'Search Horse'; these could be flown clockwise or anti-clockwise. While the squadron was changing role, a new CO took over, Lt-Kol Fiedeldij leaving on the 12th for Sydney after handing over to Lt-Kol J Zomer, a former liaison officer at Singapore. Despite the losses early in the month, no further losses were reported until the end of June, during which about 70 sorties were carried out. July was free of loss even though some B-25s were damaged by anti-aircraft fire. One Mitchell, N5-131, captained by 1/Lt Rab, was attacked by a Japanese fighter during a raid on Penfoei on the 11th but no result was reported by either side. August was likewise free of losses, even though Japanese fighters remained a real threat, something all crews had to remember. On 6 August, while proceeding for a low-level shipping recce on Lautem West, 1/Lt Rab, this time in N5-148, was forced to jettison his bombs after he was intercepted by seven 'Zekes' eight miles from the target. He found cover in cloud before the fighters were able to fire on the B-25, but the op was over and the B-25 returned to base; the Japanese had accomplished their mission of protecting their base. Another interception was made a week later on the 14th which led to a direct confrontation while attacking Ambon; Sgt Brinkman and crew in N5-128 sustained six attacks but succeeded in damaging one of the attackers, a twin-engine fighter. A few days later, on the 18th, it was the turn of Sgt Birkman and crew in N5-149 to be intercepted by two Japanese fighters during an attack of Koepang. Birkman was forced to jettison his bombs into the sea and managed to evade by diving from 8,000 feet, although the Japanese only gave up after ten

Still wearing its US serial on the tail, this B-25, wearing the Dutch flag, has yet to have its Dutch serial painted on. N5-168 was later handed over to the RAAF as A47-35.

The three Dutch officers who succeeded Fiedeldij at the head of No. 18 (NEI) Squadron, Lt-Kol J.J. Zomer, Lt-Kol E.J.G. Te Roller (killed in action on 23 June 1944) and Lt-Kol D. Asjes. Asjes survived the war with a DFC received in April 1945, the only unit CO to be so awarded

minutes of hunting the elusive Mitchell. About 80 sorties were carried out in August; the squadron's total since commencing ops was now over 500. In September, the winds of change began to blow. New crews began to be posted in, among them the first to have been trained at a joint Dutch Army–Navy flying school set up in Jackson, Mississippi. These crews brought with them their own B-25s, which were of a later variant with heavier nose armament and better equipment. Therefore, the older aircraft in use were withdrawn and some later converted to transports. From that point it became possible for the squadron to execute more efficient offensive recces, attacks on enemy vessels, harbours, airfields and other ground targets with a new internal organization consisting of four flights of four Mitchells replacing the five flights of three aircraft. After some time without sustaining any loss, October proved to be a bloody month. The first loss occurred on 7 October when N5-136, flown by Sgt C Visser, was intercepted by a Japanese fighter and shot down. Only the wireless operator, Sgt J Van Burg, survived. That was followed two weeks later when N5-156 was lost during a night bombing exercise. On returning from the range, the Mitchell caught fire and crashed about three miles east of Hughes Field. All the crew except Sgt Kleesman, who was killed in the crash, managed to bale out safely; Sgt Engels suffered a sprained ankle in the process. One more Mitchel was lost by accident on the 17th N5-145 was badly damaged after running off the runway in a downwind landing at Batchelor airfield returning from a practice flight. The crew captained by 1/Lt de Serière escaped injuries, but the Mitchell was eventually converted to components in February 1944 in regards of the damages sustained.

From November 1943, offensive tasking increased. That was achieved by a much closer cooperation with RAAF squadrons, including being escorted by Beaufighters. As a result, in the last two months of 1943, the squadron sank or left burning six Japanese ships totaling 25,545 tons, not counting numerous smaller vessels. This led to the unofficial squadron badge, the 'Dutch Cleanser' – a Dutch farm wife sweeping out dust with a large broom. During this period, the squadron lost another Mitchell, N5-159, which was shot down by anti-aircraft fire on 21 November with the loss of the crew; it was seen to crash into the sea. On the administrative side, the unit came under No. 79 Wing RAAF which had just established with one Beaufort squadron (No. 1) and two Beaufighter units (Nos. 2 and 31). No. 2 Squadron would soon convert to the Mitchell.

The new year did not start well when N5-137 was posted missing with its crew on 5 January during a shipping strike in the vicinity of Tenau. The Mitchell was seen to crash into the sea. During the same op, the Mitchell captained by 1/Lt Holswilder collided with the mast of a vessel but managed to remain airborne, continue the attack and make its way home. The B-25J with its rear turret was soon introduced, the first being taken on charge in the second half of January. By April, the new variant had almost replaced the older Ds, even though the J model was considered less maneuverable at low level. With the continued shortage of Dutch personnel, the tail position was manned by RAAF personnel. January was also the month during which the unit achieved its 1000th Mitchell sortie. The squadron sustained its second loss of the year on 7 March when N5-179 failed to return from its first sortie during a night strike on Toeal Islands. In March, based on information obtained shortly before, Allied authorities suspected Japanese forces had planned an invasion of the west coast of Australia. This resulted in the decision to take certain precautions and a deployment was ordered, the squadron leaving for Potshot on Exmouth Gulf on 10 March. After two weeks, the deployment ended when it was found the Japanese would not be invading; the squadron returned to Batchelor on 23 March. Very few flights were flown during the deployment which was, in the end, a waste of time. On the return from Potshot, a change of command took place, Lt-Kol Zomer relinquishing command to Lt-Kol E Te Roller. His command was brief, however, as he was killed in action during a bombing raid off the Kai Islands on 23 June while lea-

In 1944, No. 18 (NEI) Squadron received brand new B-25Js which progressively replaced the older Ds. The D was generally favoured by the pilots as it was more agile than the J even though the newer variant was better equipped to defend against Japanese fighters, a factor that became less important as the war progressed and encounters with enemy fighters less common. Here, N5-188, a D-model is leading Js N5-218, N5-230 and N5-226 at the end of the summer of 1944 while, above, N5-230 and N5-228 are seen together.

The last two COs of No. 18 (NEI) Squadron were M. Van Haselen and R. Jessurun, who was killed after the war in the NEI in an aircraft crash on 14 May 1949. mand until December. A former Do24 unit commander in the NEI, he fought the Japanese until Java fell in March 1942. He managed to avoid capture and reached Australia. He was awarded the DSO in August 1944.

ding the squadron in N5-162. The B-25 was hit by flak, crashed into the sea and exploded, killing the crew. This loss came just a few days before the unit's 1,500th sortie. Te Roller's command was also plagued by two earlier losses, N5-177 on 21 May and N5-176 on the 30th of the same month, the latter during a low-level bombing exercise when it crashed into the sea near Grose Island off Darwin. The entire crew of six, commanded by 1/Lt R Bouché, perished. Te Roller was replaced by Lt-Kol D Asjes on 1 July, until then chief of operations. His first month of command was free of any accident or operational loss while the squadron flew more than 120 sorties. This figure approached 150 in August, but two Mitchells failed to return. On 19 August, N5-210, captained by OVL2 H Spoel, was hit by anti-aircraft fire after releasing its bombs over an airstrip near Langgoer; it burst into flames and crashed into the sea. A few days later, on 24 August, the crew of Kapt P André de la Porte was posted missing in N5-169. On 1 September, the airstrip of Langgoer was attacked again and N5-214 was lost to the defences; its crew, captained by OVL3 AA Dreher and belonging to the Dutch Navy, perished. This target was almost a curse for the Dutch as another Mitchell, N5-222, was also lost in the same circumstances on the 15th; 1/Lt Vogled and his crew did not survive either. That was the final loss of the year. In the final three months of 1944, the squadron carried out 320 sorties without major incident. In the meantime, a new CO took over, Asjes relinquishing command to Lt-Kol Van Heselen on 7 October. At the end of December, unit strength consisted of 550 personnel, roughly half of whom were Dutch. The following Mitchells were used on operations at the time: N5-165, 166, 167, 170, 188, 209, 211, 217, 221, 228, 230, 233, 234, 237 and 234; half of them were recent B-25Js,. In December N5-167 was lost when on the 19th, it caught fire while being prepared for another mission and bombs exploded. Fortunately, no one was injured and could leave the zone before the explosion.

January 1945 saw operational activity reduced with only 47 sorties recorded. Excluding the non-operational accident of N5-211 on the 8th, which crashed on take-off causing no casualties, the start of the new year was uneventful. The squadron continued to carry out anti-shipping strikes around the island of Timor, sometimes operating from Truscott airfield. However, up to the end of April, just over 110 sorties had been flown for the period; fortunately, no losses, accidental or operational, were reported. One major operation was flown on 6 April when a Japanese convoy, whose escort included the light cruiser Isuzu, was discovered in the Flores Sea, apparently evacuating troops from Timor. The squadron participated in the attack with ten B-24s from No. 21 Squadron RAAF (see *SQUADRONS!* 28) and the Dutch managed to score two direct hits on the light cruiser. On 17 July, the squadron moved to Balikpapan on Borneo under the command of a new CO, Lt-Kol R Jessurun who had stepped into the role the previous 13 June (he had been seriously injured in the crash of N5-152 on 22 May 1943). After arriving at Balikpapan, the unit's main task was to drop propaganda leaflets and locate, and drop supplies to, Allied personnel in prison camps throughout the NEI, re-equipping with brand-new B-25Js at the same time. It also provided support to an Australian amphibious landing on Makassar in late September 1945 after the cessation of hostilities with Japan. On 2 September, the Empire of Japan surrendered. Sadly, two days later, on the 4th, N5-255 crashed on take-off for a leaflet flight, killing the entire crew. With war over in the Pacific, re-organisation got underway and, on 25 November, the RAAF component of the squadron was disbanded. A few days before, N5-254 was wrecked in an accident. Two months later, the unit officially passed to Dutch control and would continue to fly against Indonesian nationalists for a couple of years. Indonesian independence saw 18 Squadron handed over to the Indonesians; it disbanded on 26 July 1950.

In addition to 18 Squadron, it is worth noting that a second Dutch B-25 squadron under RAAF command was formed to join the struggle. This unit, No. 119 (NEI), was officially formed on 1 September 1943 under the same organisational arrangement, meaning the

Australians would have to provide personnel to fill potential gaps. This unit even received its first two B-25s, N5-134 and N5-142, on 9 October. It was a premature move, however, as it was soon found that maintaining the squadron with Dutch crews over a long period of time would be impossible, as not enough were being trained to man two bomber squadrons. As a result, the squadron was disbanded on 15 November. The assigned ground crew therefore became available for No. 120 (NEI) Squadron, formed on 10 December with Curtiss P-40 Kittyhawks (see *SQUADRONS!* 59). A second Mitchell unit manned by Dutch aircrew did exist, however. Soon after, in January 1944, the NEI Transport Section was formed at Melbourne, soon followed by another section at Brisbane with, at first, Lockheed Lodestars but war-weary B-25s soon arrived to supplement the Lodestars. They were stripped of any useless equipment, like armour, turret and guns, and roughly converted to carry personnel. The first converted were N5-128, 129, 134, 142 and 143. By the autumn of 1944, due to the increasing number of aircraft, the Melbourne section was raised to squadron status as No. 1 NEITS, absorbing the Brisbane section soon after. The B-25 became the unit's main type until the end of the war.

Claims - 18 (NEI) Squadron (Confirmed and Probable)

Date	Captain	SN	Origin	Type	Serial	Code	Nb	Cat.
18.01.43	OVL2 Hendrik **Janssen**		Kon.Marine	Zeke	**N5-131**		2.0	P
	2/Lt R.L.N. **Swane**		NEIAF		**N5-140**			
	1/Lt Albert **Oudraad**		NEIAF		**N5-133**			
19.02.43	1/Lt Willem **Winckel**		NEAIF	Zeke	**N5-129**		1.0	C
	1/Lt A. **Hagers**		NEAIF		**N5-136**			
	S/Maj Gerard **Tijmons**		NEIAF		**N5-140**			
	1/Lt Benjamin **Wetters**		NEAIF		**N5-143**			
	2/Lt Bernadus **Grummels**		NEIAF		**N5-144**			
	S/Maj **Eikelboom**		NEIAF		**N5-145**			
12.03.43	S/Maj Gerard **Tijmons**		NEIAF	Zeke	**N5-140**		1.0	P
	1/Lt A. **Hagers**		NEAIF	Zeke	**N5-137**		1.0	C
30.03.43	2/Lt R.L.N. **Swane**		NEIAF	Zeke	**N5-133**		1.0	C

Total: 6.0

Summary of the aircraft lost on Operations - 18 (NEI) Squadron

Date	Crew	S/N	Origin	Serial	Code	Fate
31.01.43	S/Maj **de Jongh**		NEAIF	**N5-139**		-
	Rest of cthe rew unrecorded					
19.02.43	2/Lt Bernadus **Grummels**		NEIAF	**N5-144**		†
	Vdrg C. **Fisscher**		NEIAF			-
	Cpl **Van der Weert**	93888	NEIAF			-
	Sgt **Hoek**	94966	NEIAF			-
	F/Sgt Ronald S. **Horridge**	Aus. 404990	RAAF			-
	F/Sgt Robert G. **Tyler**	Aus. 408892	RAAF			†
30.03.43	2/Lt R.L.N. **Swane**		NEIAF	**N5-133**		-
	1/Lt A. **de Wolf**		NEIAF			-
	2/Lt C.E. **Begeman**		NEIAF			-

Above, B-25J N5-221, at its dispersal, was issued to the Dutch in June 1944. After the war, it was converted to a strafer with a nose-gun pack. Below, B-25J N5-243 was used by No. 18 (NEI) Squadron from December 1944 until the end of war and beyond. *(AHM of WA)*

Date	Name	Number	Force	Aircraft	Status
	Sgt **Rouvroye**	93600	NEIAF		-
	Sgt William C.D. **Moore**	Aus. 412029	RAAF		-
06.04.43	S/Maj Gerard **Tijmons**	93268	NEIAF	N5-140	†
	Sgt Karel van **Bremen**	23582	NEIAF		†
	S/Maj F.J. van **Wylink**	90068	NEIAF		†
	F/Sgt Ronald J. **Hill**	Aus. 407768	RAAF		†
	Sgt George B. **Weller**	Aus. 406968	RAAF		†
28.04.43	1/Lt Albert **Oudraad**		NEIAF	N5-135	†
	2/Lt Johannes de **Knecht**		NEIAF		†
	Sgt Neville G.W. **Morris**	Aus. 414152	NEIAF		†
	Sgt Albertus de **Jongh**	92247	NEIAF		†
	Sgt Geoffrey A. **O'Hea**	Aus. 405464	RAAF		†
21.05.43	2/Lt Leendert **Bal**		NEIAF	N5-147	†
	Sgt Johannes **Hoogeveld**	95750	NEIAF		†
	1/Lt Paul **Kruijne**		NEIAF		†
	Ens. Albertus **Andela**		NEIAF		†
	Sgt Cor **Van Ginkel**	92376	NEIAF		†
	Sgt Reginald P. **Leehy**	Aus. 412068	RAAF		†
22.05.43	1/Lt A.G. **Eckels**		NEIAF	N5-152	-
	Sgt Antonius **Bouwman**	93090	NEIAF		†
	Kapt Reinier E. **Jessurun**		NEIAF		Inj.
	Sgt van der **Hyde**	97600	NEIAF		-
	F/Sgt Vernon **McLean**	Aus. 411224	RAAF		-
02.06.43	S/Maj Hendrik van den **Berg**	95521	NEIAF	N5-150	†
	Sgt Antonius **Bouwman**	93090	NEIAF		†
	F/Sgt Ronald L. **Morrison**	Aus. 401456	RAAF		†
	F/Sgt Thomas E. **Williams**	Aus. 404148	RAAF		†
	Sgt Gordon F. **Prichard**	Aus. 414160	RAAF		†
07.10.43	Sgt Cornelis **Visser**		NEIAF	N5-136	†
	Sgt Herman **De Hoog**		NEIAF		†
	1/Lt Paul **Zeijdel**		NEIAF		†
	Sgt J. **Van Burg**		NEIAF		-
	Cpl Louis **Gerards**		NEIAF		†
	Sgt Rudolf **Hoogtij***		NEIAF		†
	*extra crew				
21.11.43	Sgt Willem de **Putter**		NEIAF	N5-159	†
	1/Lt Gerrit **Paalman**		NEIAF		†
	Sgt Rokus van **Yperen**		NEIAF		†
	Sgt Mathieu van **Kan**		NEIAF		†
	Sgt W.F. **Van den Coevering**		NEIAF		†
05.01.44	Capt Adriaan **Rees**		NEIAF	N5-137	†
	Sgt Sahoer **Arsil**		NEAIF		†
	1/Lt Willem **Coedam**		NEAIF		†
	Sgt Cornelius **Gontha**		Kon.Marine		†
	Sgt **Kwee Wan Tjioe**		NEAIF		†
07.03.44	Sgt Erik **Soeterik**	217	Kon.Marine	N5-179	†
	1/Lt Bernard **Vromen**		NEIAF		†
	Sgt Willy **De Eeren**	95555	NEIAF		†
	Sgt Salomon **Bilgrai**	94720	NEIAF		†
	Cpl Leo **Rogier**	93132	NEIAF		†
	Sgt Edward R. **Howley**	Aus. 8330	RAAF		†
21.05.44	1/Lt Johann **Geerke**		NEIAF	N5-177	†
	1/Lt Ernest **Soute**		NEIAF		†
	S/Maj Frits **Belling**		NEIAF		†
	Sgt P. **Walaart**		NEAIF		-
	Sgt Louis **Heys**		NEAIF		†
	Sgt Wallace J. **Cowley**	Aus. 430644	RAAF		†
30.05.44	1/Lt Robert **Bouché**		NEIAF	N5-176	†

	1/Lt Albert **Visser**		NEIAF		†
	1/Lt Robert **Fruijn**		NEIAF		†
	Sgt Johann **Burghard**		NEIAF		†
	1/Lt **Liem Yoe Hien**		NEIAF		†
	Sgt Jeffrey D. **Crosby**	Aus. 436683	RAAF		†
26.06.44	OVL2 Hendrik **Janssen**		Kon.Marine	N5-162	†
	Lt-Kol Everdahus **Te Roller**		NEIAF		†
	OVL3 Willem **Reedijk**		Kon.Marine		†
	OVL3 Theodoor **van Lier**		Kon.Marine		†
	Sgt Gerardus **Willemse**		Kon.Marine		†
	Sgt Bernard R. **Clark**	Aus. 434926	RAAF		†
19.08.44	OVL2 Herman **Spoel**		Kon.Marine	N5-210	†
	OVL2 Pieter **van Straalen**		Kon.Marine		†
	2/Lt Christiaan **Riemens**		NEIAF		†
	Sgt Bernard **van der Linde**		NEIAF		†
	Sgt Johann **van Polanen Petel**		Kon.Marine		†
	F/Sgt Douglas V. **Webley**	Aus. 434672	RAAF		†
24.08.44	Kapt Pieter **André de la Porte**		NEIAF	N5-169	†
	2/Lt Jan **Draajier**		NEIAF		†
	1/Lt Frederik **Meijer**		NEIAF		†
	Sgt Martono **Somallo**		NEIAF		†
	2/Lt Freddy **Lie Hok Hian**		NEIAF		†
	Sgt Maurice E. **Trimnell**	Aus. 436623	RAAF		†
01.09.44	OVL2 Augustus **Dreher**		Kon.Marine	N5-214	†
	OVL3 Annes **Donk**		Kon.Marine		†
	OVL3 Waldemar **Franken**		Kon.Marine		†
	Ltz Gerard **Lugt**		Kon.Marine		†
	Sgt Robert **Marsman**		Kon.Marine		†
15.09.44	1/Lt Karl **Vogler**		NEIAF	N5-222	†
	1/Lt Willy **Scholte**		NEAIF		†
	1/Lt Hendrik **van Rennesse**		NEAIF		†
	Sgt R. **de Rosario**		NEAIF		†
	Sgt F. **Engelsman**		NEAIF		†
	F/Sgt David B.E. **Bacon**	Aus. 434190	RAAF		†

Total: 18

B-25D N5-208 before being issued to the squadron in April 1944. It belonged to the last batch of D-models which had a tail turret with a single 0.50-in machine gun (see photo on the next page).
(AHM of WA)

Interesting close-up photo showing the tail turret of a B-25D as operated by the RAAF. This turret appeared on late batch D-30 and D-35 aircraft and was sometimes retrofitted to earlier models. It was more comfortable for the gunner but did not offer improved firepower, still having only a single .50 inch machine gun. Nevertheless the aiming was easier comparing to the previous installation. *(AHM of WA)*

Summary of the aircraft lost by accident - 18 (NEI) Squadron

Date	Crew	S/N	Origin	Serial	Code	Fate
05.02.43	S/Maj Louis **SCHALK**	34	NEIAF	N5-132		†
	Sgt Cornelis **HIELE**	95845	NEIAF			†
	Sgt Jan **JANSSEN**	92766	NEIAF			†
	Sgt David L. **MCPHERSON**	Aus. 408910	RAAF			†
	Sgt Harold O. **WALTON**	Aus. 408894	RAAF			†

Also on board, the following mechanics, Sgt. Major Napoleon Kessels, Sgt Andreas Maarschalkerweerd, Sgt Geert Abeleven, all NEIAF and LAC Max T. Palamo intain (RAAF) perished in the crash.

Date	Crew	S/N	Origin	Serial	Code	Fate
17.10.43	1/Lt DE **SERIERE**		NEAIF	N5-145		-

Rest of the crew unrecorded but uninjured.

Date	Crew	S/N	Origin	Serial	Code	Fate
21.10.43	Sgt **ENGELS**		NEAIF	N5-156		-
	Sgt **HOFLAND**		NEAIF			-
	1/Lt **ZIJDEVELDT**		NEIAF			-
	Sgt **KERDIJK**		NEIAF			-
	S/Maj Cornelius **KEESMAAT**		NEIAF			†
19.12.44	*Ground accident*		-	N5-167		-
08.01.45	*No details available*			N5-211		
04.09.45	1/Lt Peter DE **VOS**		NEIAF	N5-255		†
	S/Maj William DE **BRUYN**		NEIAF			†
	1/Lt Peter **WALLIN**		NEIAF			†
	Sgt Conierie **MARIE**		NEIAF			†
	S/Maj Maurits **COUWENBERG**		NEIAF			†
	F/Sgt Joseph P. **BOURKE**	Aus. 142538	RAAF			†

Was also on board W/O Argur H. Sloane (RAAF), Clerk general.

Total: 6

Number of sorties: *ca.* **1,000**

First operational sortie:
11.06.44
Last operational sortie:
25.09.45

Number of claims: *nil*

Total aircraft written-off: 14

Aircraft lost on operations: 7
Aircraft lost in accidents: 7

Squadron code letters:
KO

COMMANDING OFFICERS

W/C Leslie A. INGRAM	AUS. 379	RAAF	...	20.07.44
W/C David W.I. CAMPBELL	AUS. 250528	RAAF	20.07.44	29.11.44
W/C Thomas S. INGLEDEW	AUS. 139	RAAF	29.11.44	31.05.45
W/C Lloyd A. DOUGLAS	AUS. 403	RAAF	31.05.45	...

SQUADRON USAGE

The RAAF's use of the B-25 was directly connected to the Dutch who had ordered 162 Mitchells to replace their ageing Martin 166 bombers operated by NEIAF squadrons in the Netherlands East Indies. The occupation of the Dutch colonies in the Far East by the Japanese in 1942 prevented any deliveries being made. Although five aircraft were sent in great haste early that year, they failed to reach their destination before NEI forces capitulated in March 1942. Meanwhile, many NEIAF airmen had been eva-cuated to Australia and the possibility of forming RAAF squadrons manned by the Dutch airmen was discussed; an agreement was reached whereby two squadrons would be formed, one fighter and one bomber. These units would become NEIAF units under the full control of the RAAF. Regarding the bomber force, it was logical to equip this unit, No. 18 (NEI) Squadron, with the Mitchell as they had been paid for and the Dutch did not want them charged to their Lend-Lease account in the USA. The first Mitchells taken on charge by the Dutch arrived in April 1942 on loan from the USAAF. Over the following years, no less than 150 B-25s were delivered and soon there were too many for a single squadron to operate.

The idea of a second bomber squadron was stillborn due to the shortage of Dutch aircrew; the NEIAF eventually transferred a number of B-25s to the RAAF, the first deliveries occurring in May 1944. The RAAF received a mixed batch of the more recent sub-types of the B-25D and early sub-types of the J. In all, 39 NEIAF Mitchells were transferred to the RAAF to equip No. 2 Squadron, the only Australian combat unit to operate the type. All the aircraft were in good condition, with low hours on their airframes, and none had seen service with 18 Squadron. For stores purposes, the RAAF allocated the airframe number 'A47' to their B-25s, this prefix forming part of the serial number, and all were modified to RAAF standards.

On 23 January 1945, the Australians reached an agreement, Requisition No. 43336, for a batch of brand-new B-25Js to be deli-vered from the United States but these were terminated after the receipt of the 11th aircraft. The exact number of Lend-Lease B-25s scheduled to be supplied by the Americans is not known, but it is possible the request was made to replace the entire fleet, which was now ageing and had suffered a high attrition rate, with new aircraft. In all, 50 B-25s were recorded in the RAAF's inventory, 39 of them taken on charge by No. 2 Squadron or used for training purposes. With the re-equipment of 2 Squadron, No. 79 Wing could deploy a significant force of Mitchells since 18 Squadron also came under its administration; Beauforts and Beaufighters were initially also part of the wing. It was formed in December 1943 at Batchelor, Northern Territory, as part of North Western Area Command. No. 79 Wing took part in the New Guinea and North Western Area Campaigns during 1944–45, eventually transferring to Balikpapan in the Dutch East Indies as the Allies advanced northward. By the end of the Pacific War, the wing was attached to the 1st Tactical Air Force and made up of Nos. 2 and 18 (NEI) Squadrons. The latter transferred to the

A No. 2 Squadron Mitchell, coded 'KO-G', in the early stages of the Australian use of the type. Note that all B-25Ds had a modified tail turret.

Netherlands Air Force in late 1945, while the former returned to Australia where it disbanded the following year. No. 79 Headquarters itself disbanded in October 1945, soon after the end of hostilities.

On 22 May 1944, 2 Squadron flew its last Beaufort sortie and was withdrawn from operations to convert to its new aircraft; it remained at Hughes, the base from which it had been operating since April 1943. The squadron was under the command of W/C L.A. Ingram, a regular Air Force officer, who had previously served with Nos. 14, 13 and 100 Squadrons RAAF. Mitchells brought about many changes in flying and operational procedures and the crews had to learn to work with a six-man crew instead of four, which was the usual number for a Beaufort crew. The newcomers were a second pilot and a rear gunner.

The first batch of 20 B-25Ds was collected from the Dutch on 21 and 22 April and with them came three Dutch pilots from 18 Squadron to help the squadron's pilots through the conversion. However, the Australians had considerable experience on twin-engine aircraft and, as the Mitchell was easy to fly, the conversion was completed without any major incident and the squadron became operational in less than three weeks. However, Mitchell A47-20 was damaged in an accident on 17 May. When the pilot, F/L Nelson Hill, was preparing to land, it was discovered the undercarriage would not extend due to the complete failure of the hydraulic system; there was no alternative but to belly land the aircraft. While this was successful, the Mitchell had to be sent away for repairs and was the victim of a ground accident on 1 June which resulted in it being converted to components.

The RAAF, now having two B-25 units under its command, operated both of them under the authority of No. 79 Wing, but for a time the Dutch squadron was based at Truscott. The first operational sortie was a search mission on which two Mitchells were dispatched on 11 June. The first to take off was Ingram and his crew flying A47-13 while the other B-25, A47-7, captained by S/L Alan Hayes, took off five minutes later. Both aircraft returned to base after more than five hours in the air. On 23 June, S/L Loneragan arrived to replace Hayes who was posted south on completion of his tour. Loneragan arrived in time for the B-25s' first offensive operation on 27 June. The target was the landing strip of Lautem West (Timor); nine Mitchells led by F/L Hill were involved in this action. Each aircraft dropped seven 500-lb bombs from 10,000 feet and, despite moderate to heavy ack-ack encountered over the target, all aircraft returned to base safely. The following day, a bombing and strafing mission was carried out on Doka–Barat airstrip with the formation led by F/O Joe Simpson in A47-16. On the last day of June, a shipping sweep was carried out by three Mitchells led by S/L Joe Lee (A47-3) after a fourth aircraft, A47-7, flown by F/O CJL Fileman, was withdrawn from the op at the last minute. One auxiliary sloop was strafed and left sinking; this was the first success recorded by the Australian Mitchells.

SUGAR DIVISION
(Stack Aft)

 4 STACK AFT

SUGAR ABLE

Catwalks and No Hatches	7000/10500 G.T.
Foremast Centered in Forward Well	12K 19K

SUGAR BAKER

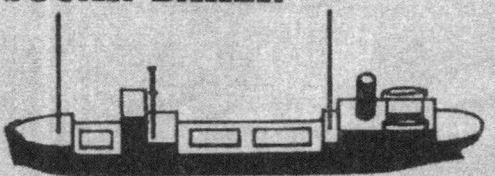

Hatches and No Catwalk	1500/2500 G.T.
Foremast usually on Forecastle	10K 13K

SUGAR CHARLIE

No Bridge Amidships	300/700 G.T.
2 Hatches, usually 2 Masts	

SUGAR DOG

No Bridge Amidships	70/150 G.T.
1 Hatch, 1 Mast	

SUGAR 2 STACKS

Stacks Abreast	17000/19000 G.T.
Slipway in Stern	13K 15K

In July, the anti-shipping sweeps continued. On the 4th, three Mitchells led by F/L John Ditchburn and crew (A47-13) attacked a 600-ton vessel not far from the Kai Islands. Bombs were dropped without any result and the 5,500 rounds of ammunition fired did not achieve anything better. The vessel continued on its way even though smoke was seen rising from its superstructure. It was able to escape a second attack due to the onset of darkness. The same day, S/L Loneragan left the squadron, on posting to No. 1 Squadron, while S/L Lee was appointed in temporary command of the squadron when W/C Ingram departed a few days later on completion of his tour. The new CO, W/C DWI Campbell, who was one of the first RAAF pilots to be awarded a DFC in the war against Japan, arrived on the 11th and officially assumed command on the 20th. Meanwhile, the squadron was able to record another success on the 15th when a motorised barge was sunk. On 19 July, during another shipping sweep, A47-15 (P/O Arthur Pierce) was damaged by flak and the navigator, W/O 'Paddy' Ryan, and waist gunner, W/O Vic Muir, were wounded; sadly, the squadron had to record its first loss when W/O Ian McCallum, the turret gunner, was killed Later that day, another raid was conducted north of Dili and yet another Mitchell (A47-15, F/Sgt Peter Hocking), was hit, and F/Sgt Jack Purcell, one of the gunners, was injured. However, the attack against the ships was not in vain as one was sunk by Sgt Hocking who was awarded a DFM for this action. From that time on, 2 Squadron regularly flew joint operations with the Dutch Mitchells. At the end of the month, the unit's situation was not the best as it only had 17 Mitchells on strength, out of an establishment of 20 aircraft, of which only 12 were serviceable.

In August, more combined operations were conducted with the Dutch. On the 2nd, an operation against Timor met with success. This raid was carried out by 27 Mitchells, including 12 from the Australian squadron. When not on operations, the Australians continued training and, during one such flight, on 6 August, A47-13, flown by F/O Stan Davies, experienced difficulty in releasing its bombs while carrying out medium-level formation bombing practice on a range. It appears that, after the bombs had been released, one exploded beneath the aircraft, setting it on fire. The B-25 crash landed in a wooded area ten miles east of Adelaide River and was destroyed. Four men, including F/O KJ Hadley, one of No. 549 Squadron's officers who had been flying as an observer, were killed outright. The other crew members, including the captain, were admitted to hospital badly burned and in a state of shock. The navigator, P/O David Lane, died four days later from his injuries and the second pilot, P/O Arthur Buckland, passed away on 19 August. This was the first Mitchell loss sustained by the RAAF. The squadron carried out about 120 sorties during the month which were mainly shipping sweeps. However, some conventional attacks were organised including one on Langgoer airfield by 11 Mitchells on 26 August. Led by F/L Philip Squires, this op called for a maximum effort by 2 Squadron and although two Mitchells were hit by anti-aircraft fire, all made it back and no one was injured.

September began with a raid carried out in the early hours of the 1st by eight Mitchells, led by the CO, W/C Campbell, in co-ordi-

A47-5/KO-N was one of the first Mitchells taken on charge by No. 2 Squadron and remained in service until the unit was disbanded.

An air-to-air shot of KO-D/A47-29, the only known Australian Mitchell to have received a shark's mouth.

nation with the Dutch squadron. The raid soon proved to be a dramatic one when A47-12, flown by F/L WA 'Tige' Carter, was posted missing. The aircraft had been damaged by flak and developed a fuel leak. When his flight instruments also failed, Carter realised he would not be able to return to base so he ditched the aircraft near a beach on the Peron Islands, which resulted in the rear gunner being injured; all returned to the squadron. In addition, 18 Squadron lost N5-214 flown by Lt Drecher. The following day, a rescue mission was launched to find A47-12 and one of the aircraft, A47-6, was also forced to ditch near the Peron Islands. Flight Lieutenant HC Easton, a chaplain on board as a passenger, was killed while W/O GSJ King, a ground crewman who volunteered to participate in the search, was posted missing. The rest of the crew of A47-6 was rescued by boat.

Despite these losses, the war continued and, on 5 September, a joint operation was carried out with Spitfire VIIIs from No. 1 Fighter Wing RAAF. The operation called for a single Mitchell, in this case A47-21 flown by F/O Les Ekert and his crew, to escort, and give navigational aid to, four Spitfires from each squadron (Nos. 54, 548 and 549), with two Spitfires from No. 1 Fighter Wing, to strike an enemy camp close to Lingat village on Selaroe Island, south of Saumlaki. After the Spitfires had strafed the enemy camp, the Mitchell dropped its four 500-lb incendiary bombs despite the heavy anti-aircraft fire directed at it. Shipping patrols and sweeps remained the main task during September, occasionally alternating with armed reconnaissance sorties or strikes on land targets. However, it was during a shipping sweep on 22 September that 2 Squadron lost its third Mitchell for the month. During a sweep along the north coast of Timor, A47-3, flown by F/O Alan Slater, was believed to have been hit by ground fire and crashed into the sea while attacking a barge. The six men on board were killed instantly. The rest of the month was busy with nearly 40 sorties carried out and, for the first time since June, the Australians flew more sorties than the Dutch.

October was a very busy month, not because of the number of ops but because of an intensive training programme. New aircrew, who had just arrived to replace the tour-expired crews, had to be trained by 2 Squadron as there was no RAAF B-25 training unit; fortunately, all the new airmen had accumulated some time on Hudsons. As the Dutch and Australian squadrons of No. 79 Wing had to convert all their crews to Mitchells 'in house', this directly affected the number of combat operations that could be flown. Furthermore, it shortened the time between airframe and engine overhauls and wore out the aircraft faster. By the end of the month, the number of serviceable aircraft had dropped to eight, out of an establishment of 20, and sorties had been cut to a third! This low number of serviceable aircraft was also partially due to operational activity as some aircraft were being damaged on operations. For example, on the 10th, A47-22 (F/O R.M. Ingram) was able to return safely to base but the aircraft was unserviceable for the next six weeks. October was also generally uneventful due to a lack of targets.

Once the new crews became operational, the number of sorties increased in November to the 'normal' level with about 100 flown. After weeks of anti-shipping strikes, the Japanese were suffering heavily from attacks by the Dutch and Australian B-25s and only small craft were being regularly encountered. Despite this, danger was still present on every sortie and A47-8 was shot down by ground fire on the 4th. The Mitchell, flown by F/L JH Selway, was hit in the starboard engine while strafing some barges. The pilot tried to pull up, but it was too late; the aircraft rolled and dived into the sea in flames, giving the crew no chance of survival. Two days later, the Australians, during a co-ordinated attack involving four 2 Squadron Mitchells and 12 more from 18 Squadron, had their revenge when they badly damaged a 300-ton ship. During the month, the Mitchells concentrated their anti-shipping activities in the Flores–Timor area with excellent results; no less than 32 vessels, including four freighters, were reported damaged or sunk and, additionally, on 28 November, they sank an 80-ton vessel. A change of command occurred the same day when W/C Campbell was replaced by W/C T.S. Ingledew, a permanent Air Force officer. Aircraft and spare parts remained in short supply and almost half of the aircraft were unserviceable.

On 5 December, three Mitchells took off on a shipping sweep not far from the north coast of Timor. While over Laga on the north coast, A47-11 (F/L Norriss and crew) was holed by heavy machine gun or 20-mm cannon fire. Fuel was seen pouring from the trailing edge of the starboard wing and the pilot immediately feathered the propeller and stopped the starboard engine to prevent a fire. However, A47-11's problems continued when the generator on the port engine failed, making it impossible to transfer fuel from the starboard fuel tanks to the port wing tanks. It was then obvious the aircraft would not be able to return to base; it got as far as Bathurst Island before the port engine stopped. Norriss made a successful crash landing despite being unable to use the flaps as the hydraulic system had also failed. Fortunately, none of the crew were injured.

On 20 December, A47-33 (F/L WFE Thompson and crew) was detailed to carry out a shipping reconnaissance but failed to return. Post-war, it was established the Mitchell had been shot down by anti-aircraft gunfire at Saumlaki. There were no survivors; among the missing aircrew was W/O J.E.S. Thompson, a New Zealander serving with the RAAF. Six days later, two other Mitchells were lost. A47-9, flown by F/O Bob Avery, was one of a formation of four aircraft ordered to take part in a strike against enemy shipping near the Lucipara Islands. This aircraft was the third to take off; the two previous aircraft had made abnormally long runs before becoming airborne, having had to use extra boost to do so. Avery was less fortunate and crashed just past the end of the runway, but the crew escaped unhurt. The aircraft burnt out and the bombs exploded, throwing pieces of metal 400 metres in all directions. This, however, was not the end of the Australians' problems for the day as the rest of the formation, led by F/L Ekert in A47-2, continued on and attacked a 300-ton vessel near the Lucipara Islands and left it severely damaged. On the way back, A47-2 was caught by a storm. Ekert commenced his landing circuit but, as he came down to 50 feet, visibility dramatically deteriorated. Ekert had no option but to continue his landing; the aircraft overshot the runway and cra-

Three B-25s in formation in the early stages of the type's operational service with No. 2 Squadron. Here, A47-14/KO-F is seen in standard camouflage, inherited from the Dutch, while wearing the markings painted on RAAF Mitchells at the beginning of their operational service.

Mitchell A47-16/KO-L flying at ground level over a river.

shed. With two Mitchells lost that day the Australians had suffered a 50% loss rate without any direct enemy action. A47-9 and A47-2 were the last two operational Mitchell losses for the month; in all, four 2 Squadron aircraft were lost in December across 108 sorties. These losses could be considered high if compared with the results: four freighters and 25 smaller vessels claimed as destroyed by No. 79 Wing. The Dutch lost just one Mitchell, N5-167, across 82 sorties.

In January 1945, the squadron began preparing to move to Jacquinot Bay in eastern New Britain with the rest of the wing to provide air support for the ongoing Army operations in that sector. This move had become necessary because the success of the operations carried out during the previous months by the two Mitchell squadrons had forced the Japanese to cease all shipping activities in the area of No. 79 Wing's operations. The proposed move affected the squadron's operations and only 100 sorties were recorded during the first two months of 1945. Meanwhile, the move to New Britain proved chaotic due to a lack of shipping to transport the wing to its new base at Jacquinot Bay. In addition, the facilities had not yet been modified to accommodate the Mitchells. An advance party arrived at Jacquinot Bay at the end of February and by late March nearly half the ground staff and most of the squadron's ground equipment had left Hughes. However, at that time, the advance of American forces in the area obliged the Dutch authorities to request 79 Wing be used on Dutch territory. Indeed, it was politically important for the Dutch to have their two units, 18 Squadron, and No. 120 (NEI) Squadron (see *SQUADRONS! 59*) with its P-40s, which had recently arrived to join the wing, operate from NEI territory. Consequently, on 14 May the move to Jacquinot Bay was cancelled and the wing received new orders to move to Morotai for assignment to the 1st Tactical Air Force in Borneo. Meanwhile, and before the move took place, operations continued to slow and no operational flights were recorded in May. With a lack of targets, the Mitchell crews were rarely required for operations. They were occasionally called upon to provide air cover for air–sea rescue searches, a tasking which could be dangerous. On one such sortie, on 28 April, A47-39, flown by F/L James Legge, was hit by ground fire while providing cover for a Catalina attempting to locate the crew of a ditched Liberator. The Japanese fire was accurate and hit the port engine which had to be shut down. Nevertheless, Legge was able to make it back to base. On 31 May, the CO, W/C Ingledew, was posted south on completion of his tropical tour and was replaced by W/C LA 'Smoky' Douglas from No. 79 Wing HQ, who arrived that same day. Once again, the move, this time to Borneo, was protracted. The first transfer of aircraft took place on 14 August with only six Mitchells making the trip. Regrettably, one of them was lost during this flight when they encountered heavy clouds. The formation, led by F/L Neil Sharpe, had to descend below 3,000 feet and A47-37, flown by F/L Edward White, was last seen disappearing behind a cloud. Meanwhile, the formation had to descend to 1,000 feet and, because of the clouds, was forced to split up. What happened to A47-37 is not known but the wreckage of the aircraft was found years later; it was suspected the Mitchell probably hit a hill while flying into clouds. None of the eight men on board survived. This loss, the day before the Japanese surrendered, was a bitter one for the squadron.

The squadron was reunited by the end of August and, although all offensive flights had been discontinued, there was still a lot of flying to be done. Watching for Japanese activity was of great importance as no one could be sure all Japanese units would surrender; some Japanese troops could well continue hostilities even after the official surrender. Reconnaissance sorties continued to be carried out with the first taking place on 19 August. This flight was made by W/C Douglas and what many feared would happen occurred when his aircraft, A47-35, was hit by ground fire.

One of the Mitchells' new tasks was to locate the many prisoner-of-war camps in the region and drop food to them. On 15 September, 2 Squadron lost another Mitchell when A47-19, flown by F/L Lawrence Kirk, was detailed to escort a Catalina to Banjarmasin and drop leaflets to native villages en route. After the Catalina landed, the pilot of the Mitchell flew low in the vicinity of the township, apparently with the idea of impressing the natives, or the Japanese, as the attitude of both was doubtful at the time. Kirk misjudged his height and the Mitchell struck a coconut tree, crashed and burst into flames, killing five of those on board on impact. Two airmen survived the crash but, sadly, Sgt FJ Stolweather died a few hours later and only the rear gunner, F/Sgt EAR Booth, survived. The last operational flight, a supply mission to Makassar, was carried out on 25 September by A47-31 and the crew of F/L George Inglis. Soon after, when it became clear the Japanese were surrendering as ordered, the ground crew removed all weapons from the Mitchells and converted them to transport aircraft. They were mainly used as a fast means of transporting Australian PoWs. On 8 October, the last accident occurred when S/L DH Hannah hit aircraft jacks on the edge of the flare path with his starboard propeller. The aircraft, A47-23, was never repaired as the authorisation to do so was not granted due to the end of the war as the Lend-Lease programme obliged the Australians to pay all costs from that date.

Once this task was completed, the squadron switched to escorting the many RAAF aircraft being returned to their new bases, or even direct to the air depots, in Australia. This chapter of the squadron's activities, and the Mitchell, ended on 14 November when flying ceased. The squadron then began its own preparations to move back to Australia with the first airlift taking place on the 23rd. All in all, 2 Squadron and its Mitchells had carried out close to 1,000 sorties, 90% of which were completed before the Japanese surrender. The cost had been high with seven B-25s lost in operations, and five others in accidents, killing a total of 44 crewmen. Compared with 18 Squadron for the same period, the losses sustained by 2 Squadron were similar.

The end of the Mitchell's service was approaching and by the end of the year 2 Squadron had been reduced to a cadre of five personnel before it eventually disbanded on 15 May 1946. By then the Mitchells were long gone, having been sent to storage depots as the type had not been selected to remain in the post-war RAAF as it was a medium bomber; the Avro Lincoln heavy bomber, which was being built in Australia, was chosen for post-war service.

Mitchell A47-11/KO-C, the only known example of a No. 2 Squadron bare-metal Mitchell to have received full squadron codes. *(AHM of WA)*

Line-up of some of the Mitchells of No. 2 Squadron: A47-7/KO-S, A47-34/KO-E, A47-37/KO-V, A47-27/KO-A and A47-19/KO-G. This photo was taken at Hughes Field in the Northern Territory on 19 July 1945 where they were used in anti-shipping sweeps in the Netherlands East Indies with considerable success. In July 1945, the squadron was preparing to move forward after months of inactivity, but the sudden end of the war altered those plans. *(AHM of WA)*

Although 2 Squadron was the only frontline RAAF unit to operate the Mitchell, some of the aircraft were also flown by second-line units. The principal one was the Central Flying School (CFS) at Point Cook which was in charge of training RAAF instructors and setting standards for RAAF pilots. For this purpose, four Mitchells were issued to CFS at various times. The first two, A47-38 and 39, were delivered in October 1944, however A47-39 only remained for a month before it was issued to 2 Squadron. A47-38, which remained on strength until April 1946, was joined by A47-30 on 7 October 1945 and A47-50 in January 1946. The latter remained with CFS until May 1946 and was the last Mitchell still flying with an RAAF unit.

Prior to arriving at CFS, A47-30 had served with No. 1 Aircraft Performance Unit (1 APU) since March 1945. An example of each aircraft type in service, or considered for service, with the RAAF had to be assessed by this unit which included among its tasks defining the flying characteristics of each type and production of a flight manual for use by RAAF personnel. In addition, it conducted tests on modified aircraft and individual pieces of equipment. A47-30 trialled new bombsights and was used to conduct armament trials for B-25Js. A47-40, in which SCR-729 radar equipment had been installed, was the second aircraft to be issued to 1 APU, but its service with the unit was brief as, five days later, it crashed just outside of the airfield boundary immediately after take-off, wrecking the aircraft without causing serious injuries to the crew. The pilot, F/L JAB Boyd, had just 2.5 hours on Mitchells and his lack of experience on the type might well have been part, if not the main cause, of the reason behind the accident. Otherwise, all Mitchells which were not immediately issued to squadrons were held at the air depots, usually Nos. 1 or 3 AD, where flight tests were occasionally flown to check their airworthiness. On 11 December 1944, F/L Robert Wines was carrying out an armament test flight in A47-24 when it caught fire and crashed into the sea off Torquay firing range. Three crew members were killed including Wines, an experienced pilot who had been awarded the DFC in 1943 while flying Bostons with No. 22 Squadron.

As the Mitchells were not selected to remain in the RAAF's post-war inventory, they were rapidly withdrawn from service and put into storage awaiting disposal; all surviving airframes were officially struck off charge on 1 October 1946. They remained in storage until March 1950 when they were sold for scrap.

The Mitchell did not play a major role in the RAAF's war against Japan; the strong connection with the Dutch overshadowed Australian use of the type. Thus, its impact on the RAAF's history was not significant. Nevertheless, the aircraft and its crews carried out a successful war against the Japanese.

Date	Crew	S/N	Origin	Serial	Code	Fate
01.09.44	F/L Walter A. CARTER	AUS. 415098	RAAF	**A47-12**	KO-B	-
	W/O Reginald J. PASS	AUS. 16940	RAAF			-
	Sgt Neville R. ELGAR	AUS. 409099	RAAF			-
	F/Sgt Samuel G. MOORE	AUS. 428049	RAAF			-
	W/O Raymond ROGERS	AUS. 416790	RAAF			-
	Sgt Alfred R. BATTEN	AUS.438308	RAAF			-
02.09.44	F/L John C. SIMPSON	AUS. 400558	RAAF	**A47-6**	KO-P	-
	W/O Keith R. MILLIGAN	AUS. 406945	RAAF			-
	F/O Vincent PETERS	AUS. 401016	RAAF			-
	F/L Alfred J. HIGGINS	AUS. 416335	RAAF			-
	F/O Robert L. PARK	AUS. 418871	RAAF			-
	W/O Gordon S. KING [1]	AUS. 4795	RAAF			†
	F/L Hilford C. EASTON [2]	AUS. 423197	RAAF			†
22.09.44	F/O Allen W. SLATER	AUS. 414849	RAAF	**A47-3**	KO-Y	†
	F/O Murray S. MILLETT	AUS. 426641	RAAF			†
	F/O John F. DAGGETT	AUS. 434341	RAAF			†
	F/O Bernard A. WISNIEWSKI	AUS. 423966	RAAF			†
	F/Sgt Keith R. PHILIPSON	AUS. 429669	RAAF			†
	Sgt Desmond F. HARBERGER	AUS. 435448	RAAF			†
04.11.44	F/O Jack H. SELWAY	AUS. 403381	RAAF	**A47-8**	KO-E	†
	F/O Arthur E. POTT	AUS. 405932	RAAF			†
	P/O Harry B. WORMAN	AUS. 417438	RAAF			†
	W/O John F. STORMON	AUS. 415057	RAAF			†
	F/Sgt Albert E. HAWKINS	AUS. 418837	RAAF			†
	Sgt Richard C. PALFREYMAN	AUS. 436941	RAAF			†
05.12.44	F/L Patrick J. NORRISS	AUS. 406551	RAAF	**A47-11**	KO-C	-
	P/O Sydney R. LEGGO	AUS. 435292	RAAF			-
	F/L Philip H. UTTING	AUS. 415287	RAAF			-
	F/L Kenneth H. JAMIESON	AUS. 410160	RAAF			-
	P/O Cecil F. LYONS	AUS. 405863	RAAF			-
	F/O William J. STEELE	AUS. 412074	RAAF			-
	F/Sgt William J.E. MCGEE	AUS. 439778	RAAF			-
20.12.44	F/O William F.E. THOMPSON	AUS. 406741	RAAF	**A47-33**	KO-R	†
	F/O Leslie T. FORSYTH	AUS. 418377	RAAF			†
	W/O John E.S. THOMPSON	AUS. 415921	(NZ)/RAAF			†
	W/O Francis H. MATHEWS	AUS. 418970	RAAF			†
	F/Sgt John A. ROLFE	AUS. 432434	RAAF			†
	F/Sgt Thomas H. ROWLANDS	AUS. 419918	RAAF			†
26.12.44	F/O Robert L. AVERY	AUS. 408360	RAAF	**A47-9**	KO-V	-
	F/Sgt Thomas P. LEE	AUS. 419774	RAAF			-
	W/O Brian D. HAWTHORNE	AUS. 410662	RAAF			-
	F/Sgt Alexander G. ALLEN	AUS. 428114	RAAF			-
	F/Sgt John R. CUNNINGHAM	AUS. 430161	RAAF			-
	Sgt Noel E. HUNTER	AUS. 438333	RAAF			-
	F/L Edmund L.W. EKERT	AUS. 404499	RAAF	**A47-2**	KO-Z	-
	W/O Murray L. TUNE	AUS. 417434	RAAF			-
	F/L Leonard W. MacDONNELL	AUS. 404439	RAAF			-
	F/O John A. BICE	AUS. 403999	RAAF			-

W/O Earl L.F. **Ralph**	Aus. 408781	RAAF	-
W/O Charles A. **Derrick**	Aus. 410638	RAAF	-
F/Sgt William J. **Hensman**	Aus. 431725	RAAF	-

Total : 7

1 Armourer, was flying as extra crew.
2 Squadron's chaplain.

Left, A47-11/KO-C seen after its crash.
Below, A47-2/KO-Z became one of the last two operational losses – fortunately without casualties.

Summary of the aircraft lost by accident - all RAAF units

Date	Unit	Crew	SN	Origin	Serial	Fate
01.06.44	No.2 Sqn	*ground accident.*	-		**A47-20**	-
06.08.44	No.2 Sqn	F/O Stanley **Davies**	Aus. 415512	RAAF	**A47-13**/KO-D	-
		P/O Arthur K. **Buckland**	Aus. 7010	RAAF		†
		F/O David G. **Lane**	Aus. 416434	RAAF		†
		W/O John S McL. **Campbell**	Aus. 415227	RAAF		†
		W/O Arthur K. **Griesbach**	Aus. 415321	RAAF		†
		Sgt Frederick H. **Conaghan**	Aus. 433289	RAAF		†
		F/O Kenneth J. **Hadley***	RAF No. 131581	RAF		†
11.12.44	No.1 AD	F/L Robert A. **Wines**	Aus. 402432	RAAF	**A47-24**	†
		S/L Frederick R. **McGrill**	Aus. 575	RAAF		†
		LAC Ronald J. **Cavanagh**	Aus. 51756	RAAF		†
		LAC Denzil R. **Roberts**	Aus. 84111	RAAF		-
		F/L Albert G **Claire**	Aus. 273495	RAAF		-
14.08.45	No.2 Sqn	F/L Edward M. **White**	Aus. 402097	RAAF	**A47-37**/KO-V	†
		F/O Alban K. **Morell**	Aus. 7246	RAAF		†
		F/Sgt Bernard M. **O'Brien**	Aus. 431510	RAAF		†
		F/Sgt Roderick A. **MacGregor**	Aus. 433732	RAAF		†
		Cpl William J.C. **Maxwell**	Aus. 34759	RAAF		†
		LAC Bayard A. **Marshall**	Aus. 73231	RAAF		†
		LAC Victor A. **Morgan**	Aus. 88726	RAAF		†
		LAC Ian S. **Coleman**	Aus. 140811	RAAF		†
15.09.45	No.2 Sqn	F/L Lawrence A. **Kirk**	Aus. 407439	RAAF	**A47-19**/KO-G	†
		W/O Cecil R. **Ricketts**	Aus. 429384	RAAF		†
		F/O Leslie **Bishop**	Aus. 433889	RAAF		†
		F/Sgt Frederick J. **Stolweather**	Aus. 439530	RAAF		†
		F/Sgt Ernest A.R. **Booth**	Aus. 433083	RAAF		-
		F/O Peter A. **Taylor**	Aus. 440106	RAAF		†
		Cpl Ray O. **Byrne**	Aus. 33210	RAAF		†
		LAC Merlin S. **White**	Aus. 141075	RAAF		†
08.10.45	No.2 Sqn	S/L David H. **Hannah**	Aus. 404551	RAAF	**A47-23**/KO-M	-
		No detail reported on the crew.				
12.10.45	No.1 APU	F/L John A.B. P. **Boyd**	Aus. 400691	RAAF	**A47-40**	-
		F/L Keith H. **Taubman**	Aus. 63342	RAAF		-
		S/L Allan M. **Stewart**	Aus. 262713	RAAF		-
		W/O Alexander S. **Ross**	Aus. 205623	RAAF		-
		F/Sgt Lloyd G **Chapman**	Aus. 47229	RAAF		-
		Cpl Ivo J. **Maher**	Aus. 69951	RAAF		-

**Passsenger, pilot of No.549 Squadron, RAF.*

Total : 7

End of the road for A47-40, seen here after its mishap of 12 October 1945. *(AHM of WA)*

RAAF ALLOCATIONS

SERIALS		DATE ON SQN	DATE OFF SQN
A47-1 :	2 Sqn *[KO-Q]*	28.06.44	25.08.45
A47-2 :	2 Sqn *[KO-Z]*	06.08.44	26.12.44
A47-3 :	2 Sqn *[KO-Y]*	18.06.44	22.09.44
A47-4 :	2 Sqn *(see note*)*	13.06.45	23.01.46
A47-5 :	2 Sqn *[KO-N]*	20.05.44	01.01.46
A47-6 :	2 Sqn *[KO-P]*	03.06.44	02.09.44
A47-7 :	2 Sqn *[KO-S]*	06.06.44	04.09.45
A47-8 :	2 Sqn *[KO-E]*	18.07.44	04.11.44
A47-9 :	2 Sqn *[KO-V]*	22.05.44	26.12.44
A47-10 :	2 Sqn *[KO-W]*	26.05.44	22.11.45
A47-11 :	2 Sqn *[KO-C]*	06.07.44	05.12.44
A47-12 :	2 Sqn *[KO-B]*	12.06.44	01.09.44
A47-13 :	2 Sqn *[KO-D]*	03.06.44	06.08.44
A47-14 :	2 Sqn *[KO-F]*	27.05.44	06.12.45
A47-15 :	2 Sqn *[KO-X]*	20.05.44	19.07.44
		26.11.44	25.11.45
A47-16 :	2 Sqn *[KO-L]*	25.04.44	23.02.45
A47-17 :	2 Sqn *[KO-C]*	25.04.44	09.05.44
		10.08.44	19.03.45
A47-18 :	2 Sqn *[KO-J]*	06.06.44	25.09.45
A47-19 :	2 Sqn *[KO-G]*	26.04.44	20.11.44
		19.02.45	15.09.45
A47-20 :	2 Sqn	25.04.44	17.05.44
A47-21 :	2 Sqn *[KO-L]*	20.08.44	17.12.45

A line up taken at Sattler Field on 15 December 1944 when the Mitchells were to provide an escort for Spitfires going to Morotai. Note that the serial of 'KO-S', A47-7, is not painted on the aircraft. Other points of interest are the tail turret and its 0.50-in machine gun, visible on the first two aircraft. Behind, A47-16/KO-L. Below, A47-21/KO-L in January 1945 with 14 bomb markers painted under the cockpit. *(AHM of WA)*

Above, A47-16/KO-M seen at the end of the war, stripped of all machine guns.
Not all Australian B-25s were camouflaged and at least four were stripped to bare metal including this one, 'Z', which was A47-36. These aircraft were usually flown by formation leaders. In this case no squadrons were painted on the fuselage.
(AHM of WA)

Serial	Unit	From	To
A47-22 :	2 Sqn [KO-T]	24.07.44	10.05.45
A47-23 :	2 Sqn [KO-M]	23.07.44	25.07.44
		14.09.44	12.03.45
		13.08.45	08.10.45
A47-24 :	-		
A47-25 :	2 Sqn [KO-J]	29.07.44	05.03.45
		07.07.45	18.12.45
A47-26 :	2 Sqn [KO-K]	29.06.44	09.11.45
A47-27 :	2 Sqn [KO-A]	29.06.44	13.02.45
		24.05.45	21.12.45
A47-28 :	2 Sqn [KO-B]	07.09.44	19.02.45
		07.06.45	01.01.46
A47-29 :	2 Sqn [KO-D]	20.08.44	21.12.45
A47-30 :	1 APU	06.03.45	02.10.45
	CFS	02.10.45	16.04.46
A47-31 :	2 Sqn [KO-P]	03.09.44	21.12.45
A47-32 :	2 Sqn [KO-Y]	19.10.44	16.07.45
A47-33 :	2 Sqn [KO-R]	01.12.44	20.12.44
A47-34 :	2 Sqn [KO-E]	08.11.44	30.10.45
A47-35 :	2 Sqn [KO-R]	12.05.45	08.01.46
A47-36 :	2 Sqn [KO-Z]	22.04.45	28.02.46
A47-37 :	2 Sqn [KO-V]	22.03.45	24.08.45
A47-38 :	CFS	08.10.44	09.04.46
A47-39 :	CFS	18.10.44	18.11.44
	2 Sqn [KO-C]	06.12.44	28.04.45
A47-40 :	-		
A47-41 :	2 Sqn [KO-U]	27.06.45	01.01.46
A47-42 :	-		
A47-43 :	2 Sqn [KO-B]	26.06.45	21.12.45
A47-44 :	-		
A47-45 :	-		
A47-46 :	-		
A47-47 :	-		
A47-48 :	-		
A47-49 :	-		
A47-50 :	CFS	16.01.46	08.05.46

Note : Regarding the code letters of No.2 Squadron aircraft, these are as known from surviving photo at a time and not necessary for all the time spent at the squadron. Duplicated letter usage is due to introduction of replacement aircraft.

*A47-4 : The aircraft status card indicates that the aircaft was issued to No.2 Squadron in June 1945 only. But No.2 Squadron ORB confirmed its presence at the squadron in June 1944, probably on loan from No.2 AD.

Some nose arts painted in Australian Mitchells, A47-7/KO-S and A47-19/KO-G.
(AHM of WA)

Above, B-25 Mitchell A47-29/KO-D with its famous shark's mouth at Balikpapan, Borneo, in 1945. A47-35/KO-R can be seen in the background. Below, A47-31/KO-P seen from a three-quarter back position and giving some details on the tail. *(AHM of WA)*

Above, B-25 Mitchell A47-37/V, as no squadron codes were worn.
In the last stages of the war, the top turret and fuselage blisters were deleted to save weight. Note on KO-B/A47-43 the individual letter is repeated on the nose but painted black, not white as shown on 'KO-M'. *(AHM of WA)*

Some nose arts painted in Australian Mitchells. Above A47-27/KO-A and left A47-32/KO-Y.
(AHM of WA)

Serial	TOC	US Serial	Type	Nbr of sorties	Comment
N5-122 (2)	-	41-12437	B-25C-NA	1	ex N5-132
N5-123	-	41-12464	B-25C-NA	-	ex N5-134
N5-124	-	41-12439	B-25C-NA	6	ex N5-136
N5-125	-	41-12482	B-25C-NA	-	ex N5-151
N5-126	-	41-12501	B-25C-NA	3	ex N5-161
N5-127	-	41-12494	B-25C-NA	3	ex N5-146
N5-128	20.08.42	41-12935	B-25C-NA	62	
N5-129	24.08.42	41-12916	B-25C-NA	66	To M-329
N5-130	23.08.42	41-12914	B-25C-NA	15	
N5-131	25.08.42	41-12936	B-25C-NA	59	To M-331
N5-132	27.08.42	41-12919	B-25C-NA	14	**To N5-122** July 42
N5-133	29.08.42	41-29724	B-25D-NC	11	
N5-134	12.04.42	41-12464	B-25C-NA	6	**To N5-123** July 42
N5-134 (2)	31.08.42	41-12885	B-25C-NA	25	To M-334
N5-135	02.09.42	41-12912	B-25C-NA	15	
N5-136	12.04.42	41-12439	B-25C-NA	8	**To N5-124** July 42
N5-136 (2)	04.09.42	41-12933	B-25C-NA	55	
N5-137	06.09.42	41-29735	B-25D-NC	16	
N5-138	08.09.42	41-12934	B-25C-NA	85	
N5-139	01.04.42	41-12507	B-25C-NA	-	To RAF India April 42
N5-139 (2)	09.09.42	41-12913	B-25C-NA	2	
N5-140	01.04.42	41-12468	B-25C-NA	-	To RAF India April 42
N5-140 (2)	14.09.42	41-29723	B-25D-NC	10	
N5-141	22.09.42	41-29725	B-25D-NC	18	
N5-142	28.09.42	41-29716	B-25D-NC	-	To M-342
N5-143	01.04.42	41-12445	B-25C-NA	-	To RAF India April 42
N5-143 (2)	28.09.42	41-29722	B-25D-NC	20	
N5-144	01.04.42	41-12495	B-25C-NA	-	To RAF India April 42
N5-144 (2)	28.09.42	41-29717	B-25D-NC	4	
N5-145	01.04.42	41-12509	B-25C-NA	-	To RAF India April 42
N5-145 (2)	17.09.42	41-12798	B-25C-NA	18	
N5-146	30.06.42	41-12494	B-25C-NA	-	**To N5-127** July 42
N5-146 (2)	01.04.43	42-32512	B-25C-15-NA	80	To M-346
N5-147	01.04.43	42-32484	B-25C-15-NA	11	
N5-148	01.04.42	41-12508	B-25C-NA	-	To RAF India April 42
N5-148 (2)	03.04.43	42-32338	B-25C-10-NA	88	To M-348
N5-149	03.04.43	42-32511	B-25C-15-NA	84	To M-349
N5-150	06.04.43	42-32337	B-25C-10-NA	9	
N5-151	12.04.42	41-12482	B-25C-NA	8	**To N5-125** July 42
N5-151 (2)	06.04.43	42-32485	B-25C-15-NA	71	To M-351
N5-152	12.04.43	42-32483	B-25C-15-NA	6	
N5-153	04.05.43	42-32339	B-25C-10-NA	30	
N5-154	25.09.43	41-30584	B-25D-20-NC	15	To M-354
N5-155	28.09.43	41-30586	B-25D-20-NC	13	
N5-156	24.09.43	41-30587	B-25D-20-NC	7	
N5-157	23.09.43	41-30588	B-25D-20-NC	23	
N5-158	28.09.43	41-30589	B-25D-20-NC	22	
N5-159	24.09.43	41-30681	B-25D-20-NC	11	
N5-160	28.09.43	41-30713	B-25D-20-NC	27	To M-358
N5-161	12.04.42	41-12501	B-25C-NA	-	**To N5-126** July 42
N5-161 (2)	24.09.43	41-30816	B-25D-20-NC	13	
N5-162	10.01.44	42-87349	B-25D-25-NC	34	
N5-163	11.01.44	42-87350	B-25D-25-NC	58	To M-363
N5-164	08.04.44	42-87305	B-25D-25-NC	34	To M-364
N5-165	04.02.44	42-87595	B-25D-25-NC	75	To M-365
N5-166	27.01.44	42-87398	B-25D-25-NC	56	To M-366
N5-167	27.01.44	41-30414	B-25D-15-NC	60	
N5-168	27.01.44	41-30416	B-25D-15-NC	17+7*	**To A47-35**

N5-169	31.01.44	41-30321	B-25D-10-NC	42	
N5-170	25.02.44	42-87254	B-25D-25-NC	69	To M-370
N5-171	25.02.44	42-87255	B-25D-25-NC	24	**To A47-36**
N5-172	10.02.44	42-87256	B-25D-25-NC	53	To M-372
N5-173	24.02.44	42-87257	B-25D-25-NC	63	To M-373
N5-174	13.02.44	42-87258	B-25D-25-NC	24+1*	**To A47-37**
N5-175	24.02.44	42-87259	B-25D-25-NC	1+1*	**To A47-33**
N5-176	13.02.44	42-87313	B-25D-25-NC	19	
N5-177	10.02.44	42-87311	B-25D-25-NC	8	
N5-178	24.02.44	42-87312	B-25D-25-NC	62	To M-378
N5-179	12.02.44	42-87307	B-25D-25-NC	2	
N5-180	xx.02.44	42-87416	B-25D-25-NC	28	
N5-181	30.03.44	43-3423	B-25D-30-NC	23*	**To A47-3**
N5-182	18.02.44	42-87597	B-25D-25-NC	-	
N5-183	26.02.44	42-87607	B-25D-25-NC	37*	**To A47-1**
N5-184	15.02.44	43-3282	B-25D-30-NC	57	To M-384
N5-185	10.02.44	43-3421	B-25D-30-NC	31	To M-385
N5-186	14.02.44	42-87608	B-25D-30-NC	19*	**To A47-34**
N5-187	24.02.44	43-2422	B-25D-30-NC	31*	**To A47-2**
N5-188	26.02.44	42-87260	B-25D-30-NC	66	To M-388
N5-189	27.03.44	43-3424	B-25D-30-NC	-	**To A47-4**
N5-190	29.04.44	43-3830	B-25D-35-NC	39*	**To A47-22**
N5-191	-	43-3424	B-25D-30-NC	-	
N5-192	27.03.44	43-3426	B-25D-30-NC	38*	**To A47-5**
N5-193	30.03.44	43-3427	B-25D-30-NC	22*	**To A47-6**
N5-194	30.03.44	43-3607	B-25D-30-NC	45*	**To A47-7**
N5-195	30.03.44	43-3613	B-25D-30-NC	9*	**To A47-8**
N5-196	30.03.44	43-3621	B-25D-35-NC	32*	**To A47-9**
N5-197	30.03.44	43-3623	B-25D-35-NC	43*	**To A47-10**
N5-198	30.03.44	43-3624	B-25D-35-NC	29*	**To A47-11**
N5-199	30.03.44	43-3625	B-25D-35-NC	12*	**To A47-12**
N5-200	30.03.44	43-3626	B-25D-35-NC	19*	**To A47-13**
N5-201	30.03.44	43-3866	B-25D-35-NC	44*	**To A47-14**
N5-202	13.04.44	43-3867	B-25D-35-NC	32*	**To A47-15**
N5-203	13.04.44	43-3768	B-25D-35-NC	57*	**To A47-16**
N5-204	13.04.44	43-3769	B-25D-35-NC	24*	**To A47-17**
N5-205	13.04.44	43-3370	B-25D-35-NC	46*	**To A47-18**
N5-206	14.04.44	43-3790	B-25D-35-NC	43*	**To A47-19**
N5-207	13.04.44	43-3791	B-25D-35-NC	-	**To A47-20**
N5-208	14.04.44	43-3833	B-25D-35-NC	-	To M-408
N5-209	14.04.44	43-3835	B-25D-35-NC	29	To M-409
N5-210	25.04.44	43-3834	B-25D-35-NC	11	
N5-211	10.05.44	43-3836	B-25D-35-NC	24	
N5-212	10.05.44	43-3823	B-25D-35-NC	25*	**To A47-23**
N5-213	29.04.44	43-3789	B-25D-35-NC	35*	**To A47-21**
N5-214	01.05.44	?	B-25D-35-NC	28	
N5-215	11.05.44	43-3869	B-25D-35-NC	43*	**To A47-25**
N5-216	11.05.44	43-3867	B-25D-35-NC	1	**To A47-24**
N5-217	19.05.44	44-27925	B-25J-5-NC	41	
N5-218	22.05.44	44-27692	B-25J-1-NC	25	To M-418
N5-219	09.06.44	44-27691	B-25J-1-NC	22*	**To A47-27**
N5-220	09.06.44	44-27689	B-25J-1-NC	49*	**To A47-26**
N5-221	05.06.44	44-27688	B-25J-1-NC	51	To M-421
N5-222	21.06.44	44-27690	B-25J-1-NC	14	
N5-223	29.06.44	44-27926	B-25J-5-NC	1	To M-423
N5-224	11.07.44	44-27927	B-25J-5-NC	13*	**To A47-28**
N5-225	11.07.44	44-27928	B-25J-5-NC	33*	**To A47-29**
N5-226	06.08.44	44-27929	B-25J-5-NC	34	To M-426
N5-227	31.07.44	44-28181	B-25J-10-NC	19*	**To A47-32**
N5-228	01.08.44	44-28182	B-25J-10-NC	50	To M-428
N5-229	27.07.44	44-28185	B-25J-10-NC	-	**To A47-30**
N5-230	27.07.44	44-28184	B-25J-10-NC	50	
N5-231	27.07.44	44-28183	B-25J-10-NC	1+38*	**To A47-31**
N5-232	13.07.44	44-29021	B-25J-15-NC	-	**To A47-38**
N5-233	15.09.44	44-29022	B-25J-15-NC	19	To M-433
N5-234	19.09.44	44-29023	B-25J-15-NC	28	To M-434

N5-235	18.09.44	44-29024	B-25J-15-NC	15*	**To A47-39**
N5-236	19.09.44	44-29029	B-25J-15-NC	-	
N5-237	19.09.44	44-29030	B-25J-15-NC	26	To M-437
N5-238	25.09.44	44-29031	B-25J-15-NC	-	
N5-239	19.09.44	44-29032	B-25J-15-NC	10	To M-439
N5-240	25.09.44	44-29033	B-25J-15-NC	-	To M-440
N5-241	14.11.44	44-29034	B-25J-15-NC	-	
N5-242	25.11.44	44-29260	B-25J-20-NC	8	To M-442
N5-243	12.12.44	44-29261	B-25J-20-NC	3	To M-443
N5-244	25.11.44	44-29262	B-25J-20-NC	-	To M-444
N5-245	14.12.44	44-29262	B-25J-20-NC	2	To M-445
N5-246	10.12.44	44-26514	B-25J-20-NC	2	To M-446
N5-247	28.11.44	44-29515	B-25J-20-NC	-	To M-447
N5-248	31.12.44	44-29516	B-25J-20-NC	-	To M-448
N5-249	03.12.44	44-29517	B-25J-20-NC	-	To M-449
N5-250	27.03.45	44-30504	B-25J-25-NC	-	To M-451
N5-251	27.03.45	44-30506	B-25J-25-NC	-	To M-451
N5-252	27.03.45	44-30507	B-25J-25-NC	-	To M-452
N5-253	27.03.45	44-30508	B-25J-25-NC	-	
N5-254	19.04.45	44-30900	B-25J-25-NC	-	
N5-255	17.01.45	44-30903	B-25J-25-NC	-	
N5-256	11.05.45	44-30505	B-25J-25-NC	-	To M-456
N5-257	23.05.45	44-30391	B-25J-25-NC	-	To M-457
N5-258	30.05.45	44-30399	B-25J-25-NC	-	To M-458
N5-259	08.06.45	44-31201	B-25J-30-NC	-	To M-459
N5-260	08.06.45	44-31202	B-25J-30-NC	-	To M-460
N5-261	07.06.45	44-31203	B-25J-30-NC	-	To M-461
N5-262	10.06.45	44-31204	B-25J-30-NC	-	
N5-263	12.06.45	44-31256	B-25J-30-NC	-	To M-463
N5-264	18.06.45	44-31258	B-25J-30-NC	-	To M-464
N5-265	25.06.45	44-31259	B-25J-30-NC	-	To M-465
N5-266	20.07.45	44-30902	B-25J-25-NC	-	To M-466
A47-40	12.04.45	44-30888	B-25J-25-NC	-	
A47-41	13.04.45	44-30889	B-25J-25-NC	14*	
A47-42	13.04.45	44-30890	B-25J-25-NC	-	
A47-43	24.04.45	44-30895	B-25J-25-NC	8*	
A47-44	28.04.45	44-30896	B-25J-25-NC	-	
A47-45	01.05.45	44-30897	B-25J-25-NC	-	
A47-46	26.05.45	44-31255	B-25J-30-NC	-	
A47-47	28.05.45	44-31254	B-25J-30-NC	-	
A47-48	03.06.45	44-31253	B-25J-30-NC	-	
A47-49	19.08.45	44-86859	B-25J-30-NC	-	
A47-50	27.08.45	44-86855	B-25J-30-NC	-	

*with the RAAF

B-25 Mitchell A47-44 taken during the acceptation fight in April 1945. The war ended before it could be issued to 2 Squadron.
(AHM of WA)

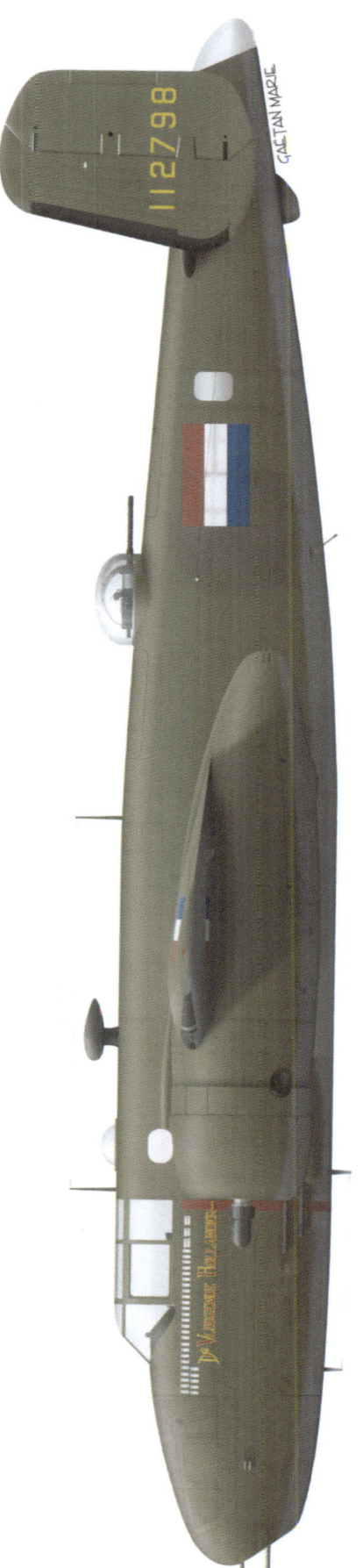

North American B-25C-NA N5-145
No. 18 (NEI) Squadron
Batchelor (NT), spring 1943

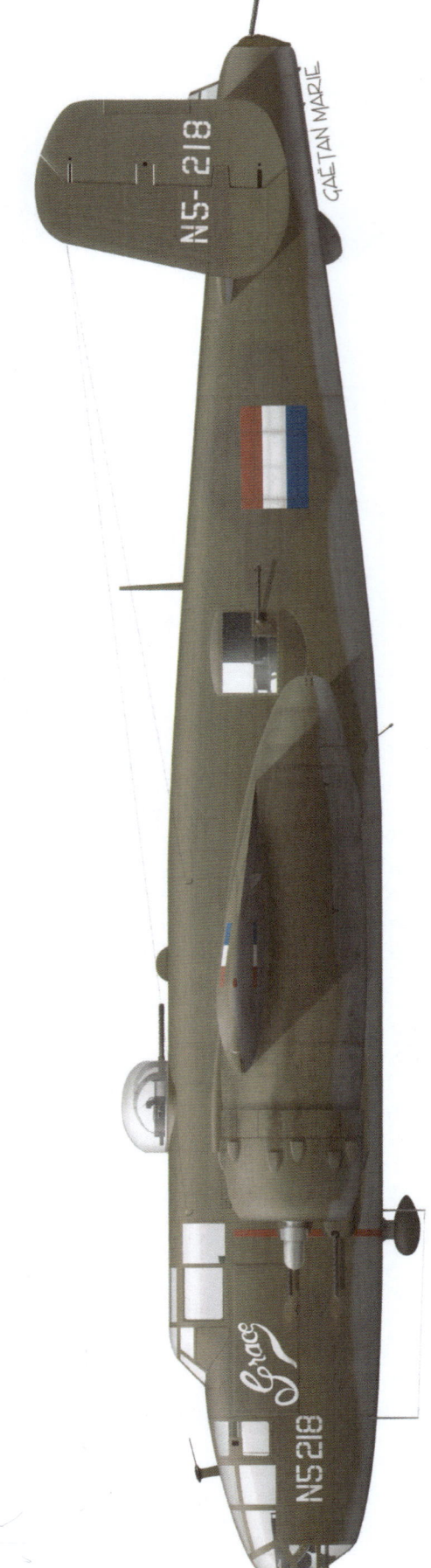

North American B-25J-1-NC N5-218
No. 18 (NEI) Squadron
Balikpapan (Borneo), summer 1945

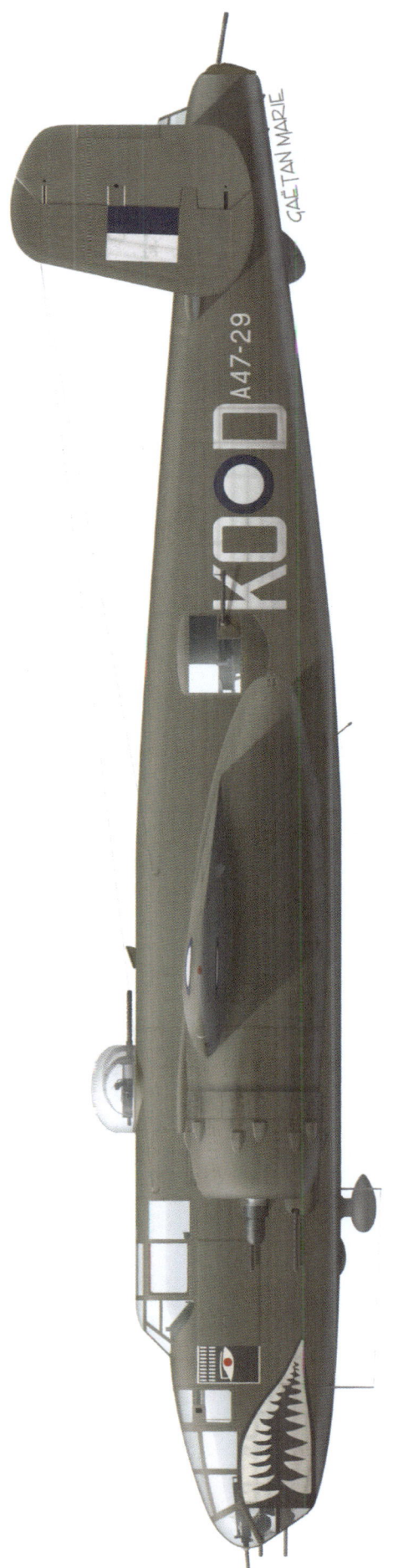

GAÉTAN MARIE

North American B-25J-5-NC A47-29
No. 2 Squadron, RAAF
Balikpapan (Borneo), summer 1945

SQUADRONS! - The series

1	The Supermarine Spitfire Mk VI		45	The Supermarine Spitfire Mk IX - *The Belgian and Dutch squadrons*
2	The Republic Thunderbolt Mk I		46	The North American & CAC Mustang - *The RAAF*
3	The Supermarine Spitfire Mk V in the Far East		47	The Westland Whirlwind
4	The Boeing Fortress Mk I		48	The Supermarine Spitfire Mk XIV - *The British squadrons*
5	The Supermarine Spitfire Mk XII		49	The Supermarine Spitfire Mk I - *The beginning (the Auxiliary squadrons)*
6	The Supermarine Spitfire Mk VII		50	The Hawker Tempest Mk V - *The New Zealanders*
7	The Supermarine Spitfire F. 21		51	The Last of the Long-Range Biplane Flying Boats
8	The Handley Page Halifax Mk I		52	The Supermarine Spitfire Mk IX - *The Former Canadian Homefront squadrons*
9	The Forgotten Fighters		53	The Hawker Hurricane Mk I & Mk II - *The Eagle squadrons*
10	The NA Mustang IV in Western Europe		54	The Hawker biplane fighters
11	The NA Mustang IV over the Balkans and Italy		55	The Supermarine Spitfire Mk IX - *The Auxiliary squadrons*
12	The Supermarine Spitfire Mk XVI - *The British*		56	The Hawker Typhoon - *The Canadian squadrons*
13	The Martin Marauder Mk I		57	The Douglas SBD - *New Zealand and France*
14	The Supermarine Spitfire Mk VIII in the Southwest Pacific - *The British*		58	The Forgotten Patrol Seaplanes
15	The Gloster Meteor F.I & F.III		59	The Dutch Fighter Squadrons - *Nos. 322 & 120 (NEI) Squadrons*
16	The NA Mitchell - *The Dutch, Poles and French*		60	The Supermarine Spitfire - *The Australian Squadrons in Western Europe and the Med*
17	The Curtiss Mohawk		61	The Belgian Fighter Squadrons - *Nos. 349 & 350 Squadrons*
18	The Curtiss Kittyhawk Mk II		62	The Supermarine Spitfire Mk I - *The beginning (the Regular squadrons)*
19	The Boulton Paul Defiant - *day and night fighter*		63	The Hawker Typhoon - *The 'Fellowship of the Bellows' squadrons*
20	The Supermarine Spitfire Mk VIII in the Southwest Pacific - *The Australians*		64	The North American Mustang Mk I & Mk II
21	The Boeing Fortress Mk II & Mk III		65	The Eagle Squadrons *Nos. 71, 121 & 133 Squadrons*
22	The Douglas Boston and Havoc - *The Australians*		66	The Handley Page Hampden *Torpedo-bomber*
23	The Republic Thunderbolt Mk II		67	The North American Mustang Mk III over Italy and the Balkans (Pt-2)
24	The Douglas Boston and Havoc - *Night fighters*		68	The Hawker Tempest Mk V - *The expansion*
25	The Supermarine Spitfire Mk V - *The Eagles*		69	The NA Mitchell - *The RAF in the Far East, the NEIAF and the RAAF*
26	The Hawker Hurricane - *The Canadians*			
27	The Supermarine Spitfire Mk V - *The 'Bombay' squadrons*			
28	The Consolidated Liberator - *The Australians*			
29	The Supermarine Spitfire Mk XVI - *The Dominions*			
30	The Supermarine Spitfire Mk V - *The Belgian and Dutch squadrons*			
31	The Supermarine Spitfire Mk V - *The New-Zealanders*			
32	The Supermarine Spitfire Mk V - *The Norwegians*			
33	The Brewster Buffalo			
34	The Supermarine Spitfire Mk II - *The Foreign squadrons*			
35	The Martin Marauder Mk II			
36	The Supermarine Spitfire Mk V - *The Special Reserve squadrons*			
37	The Supermarine Spitfire Mk XIV - *The Belgian and Dutch squadrons*			
38	The Supermarine Spitfire Mk II - *The Rhodesian, Dominion & Eagle squadrons*			
39	The Douglas Boston and Havoc - *Intruders*			
40	The North American Mustang Mk III over Italy and the Balkans (Pt-1)			
41	The Bristol Brigand			
42	The Supermarine Spitfire Mk V - *The Australians*			
43	The Hawker Typhoon - *The Rhodesian squadrons*			
44	The Supermarine Spitfire F.22 & F.24			

SQUADRONS!

No.54

Phil H. LISTEMANN

The Hawker
Biplane Fighters

AT WAR:
STUDY, HISTORY AND STATISTICS

No.137 Squadron
1941 - 1945

COMPILED BY
H. LISTEMANN
WITH
Chris THOMAS

USN AIRCRAFT
1922-1962

Vol.7:
designation Letter
'F' (Pt-4)

James Edgar JOHNSON DSO** DFC*
Supermarine Spitfire Mk.XIV MV257
No. 125 Wing
Group Captain J. E. Johnson
RAF No. 83267
B.160/Kastrup (Denmark), June 1945

www.RAF-IN-COMBAT.com

- USN Aircraft 1922-1962 -
- Squadrons! -
- RAF, Dominion and Allied squadrons at War -
- Allied Wings -
- Fighter Leaders -
- Prints (Aces and Leaders) -

Fighter Leaders
of the RAF, RAAF, RCAF, RNZAF & SAAF in WWII

Volume VII

Phil H. Listemann

ALLIED WINGS

No.19
Electric CANBERRA

SQUADRO
No.17

Phil H. LIST

The Curtiss
Mohawk

Printed in Great Britain
by Amazon

58883309R00027